RUSTON

RUSTON

FROM DREAMS TO REALITY

James D. Baker

Copyright © 2007 by Ruston-Baker Educational Institution.

Library of Congress Control Number: 2007900768
ISBN: Hardcover   978-1-4257-5678-9
           Softcover   978-1-4257-5676-5

All rights reserved. No part of this book may be reproduced or transmitted in any form or by any means, electronic or mechanical, including photocopying, recording, or by any information storage and retrieval system, without permission in writing from the copyright owner.

This book was printed in the United States of America.

CONTENTS

Introduction viii
Foreword xii
The History of the Historian xiv

PART ONE—THE CREATION OF OLD RUSTON

The Beginning: 1920-1929 2
Growth and Expansion: 1930-1946 4
Fulfillment of the Dream: 1947-1961 16
Ruston's Success 34
Factors Contributing to Ruston's Success 44

PART TWO—TOWARD CREATING A NEW RUSTON FOR THE FUTURE

Latest Chapter of the Ruston Story: 1961-2000 54
The Ruston-Baker Educational Institution (RBEI) 56
Mission and Goals of a Ruston Academy for the Future 60
What Next? 62

PART THREE—MEMORIES

Ruston in the Words of Others 66
Ruston in Pictures 124

TO ALL WHO WORKED TO CREATE OLD RUSTON AND THOSE WHO WILL TURN THE DREAM OF A NEW RUSTON FOR THE FUTURE INTO A REALITY

INTRODUCTION

This book was nearly completed prior to the author's death. My father, known as Mr. Baker by many who will read this book, had finished the initial writing process. He and my wife, Karen, were midstream in the editing process when he died in February of 2001. Years before his death, at the urging of former Ruston students, he had started thinking about writing this book. It became his final labor of love. He concluded that this book would not only have historical value, but would also serve as a guide for those wishing to carry the educational model of Ruston Academy into the future.

Jim Baker was always a dreamer. He demonstrated that dreams could come true, in large part because he was tenacious and pragmatic. This characteristic was manifested time and again in the later years of his life as he focused with other members of the Board of Directors of the Ruston-Baker Educational Institution on the definition of a new Ruston in a new Cuba. He had hoped to return to Cuba to re-open Ruston Academy himself. But, with the passage of time, he became convinced that others would need to carry the torch on that leg of the journey. He sought through the book to provide an understanding of what had made the school what it was and could be again.

Dad had wanted to use the memories of other members of the Ruston Academy family in writing this book. He had sent out a letter asking that alumni, staff, parents and friends send him their special pieces of the history of Ruston. Some did, but he did not live long enough to incorporate them into his writing. A separate section has been added to the book to share some of the memories that were shared with him. This section is rounded out with other materials that capture part of the essence of the school which he so effectively describes in *Ruston: From Dreams to Reality*.

Working on this project with Dad has given me a new understanding of much that I had taken for granted. I started at Ruston in Kindergarten in 1944 and graduated from High School in 1959. Yet I did not have a clear grasp of what made Ruston Academy so unique. I thought that it was just the way it was supposed to be. I had failed to grasp just how conscious much of what happened really was; failed to realize the degree of dedication, insight and discrete guidance which had been a central part of those who worked at the school.

Through my involvement in the project I came to realize how hard it was for Dad to try to do justice to all. A history such as this one has many unsung heroes. These range from Abuelita, who sold us our snacks, our "paleticas" and frozen candy bars, to Mario, who taught us so much about decorum through his quiet and dignified demeanor. Few of us who attended Ruston Academy are likely to forget Serafín or Generoso.

Then there are those who made the front office work, who were always there for us when we needed help. In this group I think of Sylvia Alvarez-Builla, Mariada Arensberg, Mariana Avilés, Magdalena Bradford, Noemí Booth and Berta Fontanills.

Fifteen years is a long time to spend in a school. In that period of time we benefit as students of some teachers and observe the presence and contributions of others, even though we may not have been their students. Many do not get identified in a book like this. In the first category I think of: Twyla Bryon, Silvia Carranza, Gloria Crespo, Felice Delgado, Virginia Eagan, Isabel Fernández Morell, Alicia González Recio, Ramón López, Olimpia López Laurel, Arnold Midlash, Ward Pritchett, Raquel Romeu and Colette Thurman. In the second I think of Betty Harper, Joseph Hurka, Berta Finlay, Carmen Menocal, Iluminada Pérez, Janice Pratchett, Eduardo Rexach, Rita Samson, Edith Sibert, Mary Quintero, and Sylvia Valdés Rodríguez.

To readers who did not go to Ruston, these will be unknown names lost in a listing from the past. For me, these are names of people who helped to make the Ruston that I knew, what it was. Each of us who were a part of Ruston will have a slightly different list, but all will have one thing in common: excellence.

As his collaborators, Karen and I were fascinated to watch Dad tackle this, his last "proyecto." He started this Ruston project at what he referred to as the "mature age" of 92. As he worked to make this book come to life, his love for Ruston would carry him into the very early hours of many mornings. The challenge gave him new energy and vitality. We in fact found it difficult to keep up with him. When he started to worry that he might not live to see his final Ruston effort completed, we assured him that we would make sure this book was published. The commitment is one which we hope to have carried out well, as he and the Ruston tradition so richly deserve.

To those readers who knew my father and mother, Sibyl Daker, it will seem strange that there is little in this book which describes Mother's perspective and approach to educational programs. Strange because they always operated as a team. Ruston Academy was every bit as much a part of Mother as it was of Dad. But this final effort was carried out by Dad on his own. For Mother the memory was a source of great pain. Many years before he started writing,

Dad asked Mother to write down her recollections and to describe in detail the manner in which she had put together the program for the Lower School. She could not bring herself to revisit her creative past. However, she did thrive on the reunions and looked forward to each and every one of them until her death in May of 1993.

At the last reunion dinner that Dad attended in 2000, those present acknowledged their appreciation for his contributions to them by giving him a standing ovation when he was introduced. I think that he knew it would be his last reunion. And had he chosen to speak, he might have spoken as he wrote in his yearbook note to the graduating class of 1957:

> *Some consider this a season of farewells, but to me it is a happy time. I think not of your leaving but of your taking Ruston with you wherever you may go. May her spirit and the ideals of character, personal values and citizenship which Ruston has given you remain a basic part of your future and of your life of service.*

This book is a history of Ruston Academy. But it is also a book which captures Dad and Mother's life of service to the ideals and philosophy which Hiram Ruston nurtured in so many, so well.

Chris Baker

FOREWORD

Writing this book has been very rewarding. Re-living the history of Ruston has increased my appreciation of the school's unique influence upon the lives of her students, expanded my vision of the ways in which Ruston's philosophy and values can help produce better future leaders and increased my determination to help create a new Ruston Academy dedicated to fulfilling the school's mission.

It is important that the reader realize that this "history" is based upon my personal recollection, not upon objective facts. A history should be based upon verifiable data. But much of the statistics and "facts" in this book come from my memory and that of other Rustonians. (The official records of the school were lost when Castro confiscated our Ruston Academy in 1961.)

This book records the history of the creation of a great school that had profound influences upon many students. But it is more than a record of a school's development. It is a story of how a group of educators turned their dreams of an exceptional school into reality. I hope this story will remind the reader that dreamers in any field can achieve their goals.

Ruston was produced by teams of workers, not by individuals. The credit for Ruston's success goes to all whose combined efforts over the years produced our unique Ruston!

The school shield is placed on the title page to focus attention upon an important message from Mr. Ruston. I watched Mr. Ruston design this seal. I believe that when he chose the Latin motto, "only poets know the real truth," he was saying, "Ruston will strive to help students to become poets—to understand that it is through our feelings, our relations with others, that we find life's deepest meaning."

Countless people have helped with the writing of this book. Perhaps the most important of all were the alumni who for years have urged me to write the history of Ruston. This insistence implied their confidence that I would produce the book needed. Finally, I accepted the challenge. I hope the result provides the desired record. Unfortunately I cannot name all of this group and thank them for pushing me to assume this important task.

But I do want to express my gratitude to my two assistants, my son, Chris, and his wife, Karen. Without their help my book would never have been written. They have been my advisors and aides at every stage of the production. I am grateful also to Margarita Oteiza Castro for reading my manuscript and suggesting the addition of specifics that have helped to make the Ruston story more complete. I am also particularly indebted to Mario Iglesias and Hilda Perera. I have drawn extensively upon their excellent descriptions of the teaching approaches which they introduced at Ruston Academy.

THE HISTORY OF THE HISTORIAN

Before beginning this history of Ruston, I need to explain my part in the story. I was closely associated with the school for twenty-two years, as a teacher from 1930 to 1936, as Assistant Director from 1944 to 1946 and as Headmaster from 1946 to 1961. These were the most important years of my life—the "mountain peaks" of my professional career. In 1992, my wife, Sibyl, and I initiated the establishment of Ruston-Baker Educational Institution. I have served as a member of its Board of Directors for eight years.

My part in this story began in 1930. I had graduated from Miami University in Oxford, Ohio, the year before and was working on my Master's in English at Harvard. A combination of the influences of Miami University and Harvard opened for me the door to Cuba. Mr. Ruston and President Upham of Miami had been classmates in Harvard graduate school. By some chance, in 1930, for the first and only time, Mr. Ruston wrote to Dr. Upham to see if he could recommend a teacher. Because President Upham was familiar with my work at Miami and knew I was at Harvard preparing to teach, he recommended me.

I knew nothing about Cuba, nothing about overseas schools. But at the beginning of the depression teaching positions were scarce. I accepted the offer and in September, 1930, became, in a very real sense, a part of Ruston Academy.

In 1932, Sibyl and I were married and she, too, joined Ruston. She undertook the development of a music program and taught fourth grade. We returned to the States in 1936 because we wanted to continue graduate study. Sibyl was working on her Master's in music at Northwestern University. I needed to finish my work on my M.A. in English. Mr. Ruston urged us to finish our studies and then return to Ruston. But we had other plans—we hoped to have children, and we wanted them to grow up in the States.

By 1944 we were enjoying a happy life. We had two sons, Denny five and Chris three. I had not been drafted into the army because I was serving as a housemaster at McDonough School, a boys' school near Baltimore, Maryland.

Our future was secure. Then that summer we received a long distance call from Mr. Ruston. He was in poor health and, because of World War II, was having trouble recruiting American teachers. He wanted us to return to help him and, ultimately, to become the directors of Ruston Academy.

Should we accept the offer? Sibyl and I spent hours discussing the question. We made lists of arguments pro and con. The eight years away had only increased our appreciation of Ruston's uniqueness. But the school we had known offered little financial security. We had to think of the future of Denny and Chris, as well as our own. The list of reasons for remaining in the States was long. But the single, powerful pro argument won: Ruston needed us! In August of 1944, we returned to Cuba to make Havana our home and to dedicate our lives to carrying on Ruston's mission.

From the beginning in 1930, my teaching at Ruston gave me a fuller appreciation of American values and our way of life than I would have had at home. I saw that Cuba had been strongly influenced by conquistador leaders motivated by a desire to gain wealth for themselves and their native lands. Our country had been developed by leaders who had been motivated by a different goal. They sought a new home to escape from oppression. In order to survive and to face the hardships of pioneer life, our forefathers were forced to help each other, to develop ways to cooperate in finding solutions for problems.

Understanding these two national characteristics, I saw that Ruston had a double mission—first, to develop individual students into adult contributors and second, to help them understand how to cooperate with others to find solutions for common problems.

In 2000, this second mission is more important than ever before. For forty years Castro has forced citizens of Cuba to follow his brand of communistic group cooperation. His dictatorship has reduced a once prosperous country to a subsistence economy. (In 1959, Cuba had the fourth highest standard of living in the Americas.) One of Ruston's goals throughout its existence was to help students understand and adopt the system of democratic cooperation which has produced the most prosperous economy the world has ever known. When the right time comes, Ruston needs to be there again to help produce a new Cuba based on true cooperation and freedom.

PART ONE

THE CREATION OF OLD RUSTON

THE BEGINNING
1920-1929

Opening of the School

It all began in 1919 when a Cuban student at a preparatory school in New York invited Hiram Hall Ruston, a fifty year old English teacher, to visit Havana during the summer vacation. Hiram accepted the invitation and fell in love with the beautiful island and its people. The visit changed his life completely.

Mr. Ruston was born in Princeton, Indiana, in 1869. Following completion of his high school education, he had continued his studies at Wabash College where he graduated with Phi Beta Kappa honors. He would then serve as the Principal of Princeton High School from 1895 to 1899, prior to continuing his education at Harvard University. Mr. Ruston received his Master of Arts in English Literature from Harvard in 1902. In 1901 he had joined the staff of Worcester Academy in Massachusetts where he taught English until 1907. From 1907 until 1920 he taught at the Cutler School in New York City.

Hiram's educational methods were far ahead of his time. During his years of teaching in private, preparatory schools in the East, he had dreamed of an individual-centered school that would concentrate upon helping each student develop his or her potential while making education a rich and vivid experience. Cuba offered the ideal site for his school!

Hiram returned to the States excited about his vision. During the following school year his plans to create the school were formed. He convinced his sister, Martha, six years his senior, that at last he could have his dream school. The two pooled their life savings to make the venture possible. They moved to Havana in the summer of 1920.

The school opened in September, 1920, in a spacious rented house at the corner of Calle Concepción and Avenida de Colombia (later Avenida 37 and Calle 100) in Marianao with three teachers and three students. The future seemed as bright as the sun-filled sky. The Cuban economy was thriving. The American colony in Havana was growing. There was a need for a first-class American school.

The Struggle for Survival

But clouds soon arose. Unfortunately, 1920 marked the collapse of the Dance of the Millions, the surge of prosperity for the sugar industry that had created such a bright picture the year before. Sugar prices, which had soared to unseen levels in 1919 and early 1920, came crashing down by the end of the year. As a result of this economic crisis, the anticipated enrollment did not materialize. Within a few months, the Rustons' savings were wiped out.

In 1921, forced to retrench, the Rustons moved to a small house at G y 5ta in Vedado. For ten years this house—turned into classrooms—was Ruston Academy's home.

The Rustons faced colossal financial difficulties during the '20s. The enrollment remained small. Many times they had to borrow money to pay the rent and teachers' salaries. A less idealistic or weaker man would have given up and returned to a secure position in the States. Mr. Ruston never faltered. He believed in his educational ideas and was determined to build a school that would bring these ideas to life.

Martha and Hiram made a good team. She was a tireless manager who took charge of all practical details—ran the house, collected the fees, paid the bills—so that Hiram could give his full attention to creating his new school. In one respect, they were fortunate: they owned a small business property in Indiana. That property in their hometown was their lifesaver when financial difficulties arose. It was this asset that backed the loans that kept the school operating year after year in a process of borrow, repay, and borrow again. All who later benefited from being a part of Ruston owe a great debt of gratitude to this very special brother and sister—one a dreamer and the other a practical realist.

Hiram's goal was to use his own methods to produce an elementary and secondary education similar to that provided in a very good, private school in the United States and to prepare graduates for admission to top-ranking American institutions. With over twenty years' experience teaching in eastern private schools, he had a thorough understanding of quality education.

When he founded the school, Mr. Ruston was fifty-one years old. His rugged features reflected his unusual strength of character; his eyes expressed the warmth and caring of his life-long dedication to students. Physically, in height and build, he was just an average man. But what a giant in spirit! Students and teachers fortunate enough to know him have vivid memories of him sitting in a rocking chair in the main patio, dressed in the white suit he always wore, summer and winter, and smoking the long cigars he enjoyed so much, while he dreamed of the students and the country he loved.

GROWTH AND EXPANSION
1930-1946

In 1930, the tide changed. The period of growth and expansion began. The single building grew into a plant of seven buildings. The forty students, mostly American, increased into a multi-national group of over four hundred. Instead of the beginning three teachers of 1920, there was a faculty of over fifty by 1946.

Physical Growth

For those who studied and worked in the seven unit plant of 1946, it would have been difficult to imagine the one-building school of 1930. This small house on the corner of G y 5ta had a large living room, small dining room, kitchen, four upstairs bedrooms, a large porch on one side and a patio. It provided the living facilities for the Rustons and a resident teacher and space for the classes of forty students. These multiple functions were crowded into this small space by having some areas provide several services. The living room was the school reception room during school hours, the living room later in the day, and finally Mr. Ruston's bedroom at night. The dining room served as the school office during the day and shifted to its usual function in the evening. The long, open-air porch was changed into classrooms, with a low partition separating the small space for children in grades one and two from that of the older students.

During most of the year these outdoor classrooms were very comfortable. When the occasional "norte" (cold wind from the north) blew in, the students wore thicker sweaters. And they could always warm up during recess or lunchtime by joining Mr. Ruston around his small, open, charcoal burner in the living room.

Sounds crowded, doesn't it? Yet with physical limitations that would have been intolerable later, a unique, strong, vibrant Ruston spirit grew.

By the end of the 1930-31 school year the growth in the number of students caused Mr. Ruston to begin his physical expansion. Each year between 1931 and 1935, he added another building to the house on the corner. He rented old dilapidated houses, which others considered hopeless wrecks, and remodeled them—largely by changing bedrooms into classrooms.

The second and third houses combined to make a single unit with the corner building because they were attached to it. By opening a passageway in the common walls, Mr. Ruston made them into one building.

The third house had most recently been a laundry. (In the past the noisy rattling of its antique truck as it entered or left the shop had frequently disturbed the Ruston classes held on the adjacent porch.) While this house needed extensive renovation, its addition brought an extra benefit: for the first time since he moved to Vedado, Mr. Ruston had his own bedroom!

Each summer the savings from the previous year were used to pay for the renovations. Then during the year, Mr. Ruston again had to use the Indiana property to guarantee the loans required to operate the school. A less idealistic, more practical man would have crowded the increasing students into existing space. But not Hiram Ruston! He was creating his ideal school!

This physical expansion took care of the continued increase in students between 1930 and 1946. The main unit at G y 5ta provided school offices, living space for the Rustons, resident teachers and the boy boarders, as well as classrooms for High School and Comercio classes. Two buildings, across the street, housed Primary and Intermediate classes. A block away was the Bachillerato building. Another house, half a block away, served as the home for the girl boarding students and also contained the rooms for science classes of the Upper School.

Expansion of Programs

Mr. Ruston's success with his college preparatory programs opened new horizons for him. He saw the need for well-trained, bi-lingual secretaries and bookkeepers and opened a Comercio Department in the early '30s to prepare students for work in this field. This Upper School department provided courses that developed proficiency in the two chief languages of Latin American commerce and prepared students for work in businesses concerned with Latin America.

Then, concerned because many Cuban students who wished to study at Ruston could not pass the entrance tests, Mr. Ruston added the Basic English program to provide the training in English that applicants needed.

In the early '40s, Mr. Ruston decided that the school should prepare Cuban students for admission to the University of Havana. To provide this service, he added the Bachillerato Department, which covered the programs of both Ingreso (the equivalent to the first year of junior high school, or seventh grade) and the five years of Bachillerato (the equivalent of the second year of junior high school or eighth grade and the four years of high school). This was carried out in stages with Ruston first offering Ingreso and a four year Bachillerato program and subsequently adding the fifth and final year. In the interim period, Bachillerato students wanting to qualify for admission to the University of Havana took their fifth year courses at the Instituto del Vedado which was part of the Cuban public school system.

For another expansion, Mr. Ruston turned to the opposite end of the age spectrum and opened a kindergarten class. These charming tots were his special joy. They, too, learned both English and Spanish.

Last came the boarding department. Mr. Ruston always explained that he added this facility because there were very few American programs available at the sugar mills and rural areas from where the boarding students came. But those who knew him understood that these students provided a special satisfaction for him. They were the family he never had. This program, that began with only a few students, grew rapidly. By 1946 there were ten girls who lived in a separate house and were supervised by a full-time housemother. Twelve boys lived with the Rustons in the main G y 5ta complex of three buildings. Their activities were supervised by the "officer of the day", a responsibility shared by the resident teachers.

As the programs expanded, so did the teachers. In 1946, there were over fifty teachers, more than half of whom taught only part-time. The part-time teachers were needed to cover the wide range of subjects taught and the breadth of non-academic activities offered. Some of the Bachillerato courses required teachers specialized in a particular field, who taught only two or three classes a week. The same was true of the teachers of carpentry, music, boys and girls physical education, and arts and crafts.

Cultural Expansion

Mr. Ruston expanded the school's contribution to the cultural life of students through his annual production of a Shakespearean play, sometimes a comedy, at others a tragedy. For a month every year, "the play" was the center of interest and activity. The entire school was involved. Students who were not acting gathered in the patio at noon and after school to watch rehearsals. Some painted scenery. Others created royal jewelry or designed hats. For several weeks before the play, the seamstress spent full time at the school making new costumes and adjusting old ones for new actors. In the early years when there weren't enough older boys to fill roles, the teachers were drafted. Not having an auditorium, Mr. Ruston created one by building a small stage at one end of the patio at G y 5ta. On play nights, folding chairs filled the remainder of the patio to seat the audience.

Dr. Bernard Gundlach, who taught mathematics at the school at the time, would write to a colleague many years later:

> *Thinking back to the Ruston Years, it seems to me that we happened to be there at a most unique time, when Hiram Hall Ruston was still at his prime and really ran the school (together with his disapproving sister) for the single purpose to put on plays, hopefully by Shakespeare. I will never forget our putting up the demanding Shakespearean Masterpiece "The Tempest" that he, assisted by Bill Copithorne, drilled into those gifted kids in his school, and really brought to life. Many a night I spent puzzling over the demands of an utterly inadequate electric installation and my most real fears that it might all blow up right in the middle of his beloved Patio Theater, which had in part been built before the advent of electricity.*

After Mr. Ruston's death in 1946, I continued with this Shakespeare tradition by directing a play each year from 1947 to 1959.

Student Body

When the school offerings were limited to college preparatory programs, there were only American students with a few Cubans who planned to continue their studies in the States. But with the addition of the Comercio and Bachillerato Departments, the number of Cubans increased. The existence of the Bachillerato program in the Upper School attracted more Cubans to the Lower School. As the advantages of the Lower School program became more apparent, more Cubans began their studies at Ruston. When more Cubans than Americans applied for admission to the Lower School, admission policies were established to maintain the balance of the two groups. We believed the school could best achieve its goals by seeking to have this balance.

Throughout its history, the school was fortunate to have students with varied backgrounds—the children of American and Cuban businessmen, of United States and foreign diplomats, of professionals from many countries. This cultural melting pot was enriched in the late '30s and early '40s when the influx of refugees from Europe added another strain to the mix.

Ruston "happened" in many places—when children visited historic sites, when older students attended concerts in a group, and when they met in a teacher's home on Sunday evenings to discuss contemporary problems.

Ruston meant hard work at school, but fun at other times. There were trips to the fern-filled gardens of the Hershey Sugar Mill and visits to nearby farms of Ruston families. There were class parties in different private homes. There were faculty/student games; there were picnics. The first of these picnics in the '30s was a new experience for some Cuban girls. They were surprised when they arrived dressed for a party. But they soon forgot their white dresses and sat on the grass and later waded in the small stream.

But Ruston was not an academic utopia. There were occasional discipline problems. For resident teachers, living with Mr. Ruston produced a better understanding of the philosophy of the school and a special dedication to helping implement its vision. This loyalty was reflected in 1935, when three of the resident teachers volunteered to help as a discipline committee. Mr. Ruston was at his best when inspiring students; he never liked his role as disciplinarian. So he willingly accepted this assistance. The modus operandi of the committee was to call in a student to discuss his or her inappropriate behavior. They tried to help the student find a solution for the problem that had caused the undesirable behavior. If a punishment were given, it was an assignment to Saturday morning study hall. Students referred to this process as being taken to the "dark room".

Many years later an alumna described her perspective as a strong-willed, independent fourteen year old: "I was summoned to the 'dark room' where the "ogres" met, and they proceeded to read me the riot act. I was scared and broke into tears. But those heartless three didn't even offer me a Kleenex, and I had to dry my tears with the corner of the big collar of my dress."

When we returned to Ruston in 1944, I had a number of discipline problems with the older Cuban boarders. At that time girls were carefully trained to accept strict rules. But many boys expected to have unlimited freedom. Six of the ten older boys were between sixteen and eighteen years old. They resented the restraints of a boarding school.

One time after the group showed strong reaction to the strict rules, I called in the most reasonable of the oldest boys and explained that I would be very willing to discuss the rules if the boys felt any were unfair. The reply I received was, "But, Mr. Baker, there's nothing wrong with the rules; the trouble is that you enforce them."

The leader of the "rebel boarders" was José, the son of the owner of a large sugar plantation in Camagüey, who had always been treated like a young prince in a royal kingdom. José was the instigator, if not the cause, of my being challenged to a duel.

The challenge was provoked by a strategy I had used to prevent having dances disturbed by the conduct of male guests. Guests had to be approved by me. One time I rejected a girl's date. The young man would have been suspect because he was a friend of José's. But more serious, he, as José's guest, had started a fight with another guest at a recent reception honoring Mr. Ruston. When I cancelled his name for an upcoming dance, the young man's honor was offended, and he came to challenge me to a duel. I refused to even talk with him about such utter nonsense the first time the eighteen year old came to demand "satisfaction"; I even refused to respond to the threat the second time the angry boy appeared to demand "satisfaction".

Even though duels had been outlawed for many years, one of the Cuban teachers was deeply concerned about the situation; she felt that Cuban honor would force me to accept the challenge. She feared it would lead to an international scandal and apparently had visions of headlines like "American Educator Surprised in Duel with a Cuban Student". The situation was cleared up when José's older brother, a Ruston alumnus, brought the insulted boy to me to discuss the problem. I explained that the policy of requiring approval of all male guests was set to guarantee that guests would meet Ruston's expectations. At Ruston dances all boys were expected to behave like Cuban gentlemen—no necking on the sidelines, no cheek-to-cheek dancing, no fighting. A compromise was reached; the young man could come to the dance if he agreed to behave like a Cuban gentleman. Even guests met Ruston expectations when they knew that was the price of admission.

The rebels had bragged that they were going to "drive Baker out of Ruston." Instead, they all withdrew from school at the end of the academic year.

There was an interesting sequel to this incident. Ten years later, José appeared at Ruston again. This time he was seeking a place in the kindergarten for his young son. The second generation Rustonian was accepted. I knew this was one father who understood Ruston education and wanted it for his son.

In my memory there are also wonderful examples of "misbehavior" that made us laugh. Here are two of the best.

At Ruston teachers and students had a special bond. There were times to work and times to play. One day our librarian, Raquel Romeu, left work to find that her small Renault was not in its usual parking spot. Thinking she might have parked in a different place when she came late that morning, she searched down the block. Finally she found it wedged so closely between two other cars that she couldn't move it. Some of the older boys of the Upper School had picked it up and fit it into this small open space. As she stood there trying to figure how she could solve this inexplicable problem, the boys, who had been hiding around the corner waiting to see how she would react, came out laughing and again lifted the car and placed it in the middle of the street.

The second story comes from a Comercio student of the mid-'40s.

> Mr. Felipe de la Cruz (best known by his pupils as Felipito) was the Head of the Commercial Department and our Accounting, Business Arithmetic and Business Law teacher. Minerva Armor de la Cruz was his wife and she was our shorthand and typing teacher.
>
> As we were teenagers, we thought we knew it all and of course, we didn't. When Mrs. de la Cruz was angry with us she would call us "lumbreras apagadas".

> Mr. de la Cruz liked and nearly always wore bow ties. One day, he entered the class and everybody was in their seats wearing bow ties. At first, he was amazed and when we thought he was starting to get angry, instead, he burst out laughing.
>
> We were astonished with his reaction because we thought he was going to get mad and punish us and then we all started laughing too.

The Significance of Mr. Ruston's Contribution

In the late 1970s following a Ruston Reunion in Miami, Sibyl and I sat down to write a brief history of Ruston. Though this was a joint effort, the style, clarity and poetry is clearly hers.

> Hiram H. Ruston was devoted to knowledge and sensitive to beauty in all its forms. He understood the seasons of nature and of men. Music, art, and drama spoke to him intimately. He enjoyed good conversation, and he loved laughter. He had a talent for extracting the essence from each simple experience. But he dreamed big.
>
> Mr. Ruston understood the nurture of the young, their need for freedom to grow, for self-knowledge, for inner discipline, for reaching out and up. Never condescending, he expected much of them and led them to expect much of themselves. He cherished their differences. He glorified in their gifts. He never withheld affection. Best of all, he helped them to know who they were.
>
> This educator believed in the thorough mastery of academic skills and in the importance of providing a background of knowledge wide enough and deep enough to nourish and illuminate. His students knew the discipline of hard work and the joys of achievement. They learned how to "flex the muscles of the mind," to use languages correctly and effectively, to find solutions to problems, to relate the past to the present—the present to the future.
>
> How did Mr. Ruston know so much? We can only suppose he was guided by an inner music of his own. When he died, parents looked at each other saying, "What will happen now?" But he was a superb teacher, and he had disciples. Those who had worked with him knew some of the inner music, and each played his part. Others learned.

In 1945, a jubilee was held to celebrate the Silver Anniversary of the founding of the school. It was also a tribute to Mr. Ruston. One of the clearest evidences of the scope of his dream was reflected by the tribute to him in the 1945 yearbook. The students saw him clearly! They honored him for the uniqueness of his vision for Ruston and its goals, for turning that dream into reality, for his belief in them and their work, for the challenges set for them by his ideals.

> *A quarter of a century ago an American teacher came to Cuba with a vision, a vision of a school centered around individual students and their unique needs. This dream grew into a reality, but a reality where ideals always dominated practical details and the limitations of physical conditions. His was a dream of small classes that made possible close association and friendly relationships between pupils and teachers; of a democratic spirit which made education a mutual sharing of the growth of pupils and teachers; of the development of the only true discipline, that which emanates from within the student himself. It was his desire to create an environment that would encourage students to think for themselves, to develop a capacity for self-evaluation. This teacher was more interested in the kind of mental habits students formed and the quality of trained minds they would have when they were twenty-five or forty than he was in the monthly grades. He was more concerned about the characters they would have as men or women than about their childish pranks of the present. Himself a man of wide culture, he wished to give students not an encyclopedic knowledge but culture in the true sense of deep appreciation for, and real enjoyment of, serious literature, music and art. Believing profoundly in the worth of the individual which is the basis of democracy, he saw that children could be prepared to live as citizens in a democracy only if they were trained first to accept the responsibility for themselves and their own actions. He wished to establish a school where teachers directed students as friends and exchanged ideas with them on a democratic basis. At the same time he appreciated the importance of developing in youth a consciousness of their obligations to their country and a desire to help realize its potentialities.*
>
> *With three teachers and three pupils, he began to mold his vision into a reality. Slowly the school grew. A bi-lingual commercial department was added to the regular American primary, junior high, and high school. Then came the Bachillerato and finally the kindergarten. One building after another was annexed until today the plant includes eight buildings. The faculty of three increased to forty.*

As we look back over the twenty-five years, we see that Ruston has always supported and fostered the best of Cuban traditions and aided in the development of Cuba. One of the pioneers in co-education in Cuba, the school has been very much interested in helping girls to see their responsibilities. It has always encouraged girls to continue their education in order to develop their capacities for serving their country. Ruston is proud to have as alumnae one of Cuba's first successful women architects and one of the first women to study chemical engineering.

This silver anniversary is, first of all, a tribute to you, Mr. Ruston, a tribute to your vision which has become a vital reality.

The anniversary has a double significance, however. Janus-like, we look both to the past and to the future. We still have dreams, unfulfilled dreams—dreams of a new building, well adapted to the multiple needs of our varied programs, dreams of establishing a foundation which will make permanent the educational system to which Mr. Ruston has given the best years of his life. The chief vision to which our work will be dedicated will be the continued realization of the old ideals. Never before has there been so urgent a need for the Pan-American and international understanding and cooperation which Ruston has sought to develop. The political, social, and economic trends towards bureaucracy, and the worship of groups, make it increasingly important to focus attention upon the individual, his significance, and the quality of his life.

As we face this future, Ruston shall strive to make the next twenty-five years as richly rewarding in the growth of individuals as the past quarter of a century.

Mr. Ruston's life reflected the rewards of "working to help others." If one asks, "What did he gain from his twenty-six years of tireless labor in Cuba?", the list is startlingly short. The school had provided his meals and a place to live, limited though the facilities were. During most of these years he slept on a couch in the living room of the school and had his own bedroom only in the last years. He had his white suits, his Sunday afternoon rides in the country in a rented automobile looking for the natural beauty that he loved to capture in his paintings. Yes, and his Cuban cigars, which he enjoyed as he rocked in the school patio. "Not much," one would say today. Yet Sibyl once described him as "the richest man I have ever known."

Hiram Ruston left a quiet legacy which is easy to overlook. He inculcated, both through his life and through the school, a strong commitment to values which emphasize that what counts is the person, not the trappings. The impact of his values upon the students at Ruston Academy was well captured in an article in the *Havana Post* edition of February 8, 1953.

> *Last year during the political crisis the fact that members of the families of the three outstanding political leaders were studying in the same department at Ruston presented no problem for the students involved or for their friends.*
>
> *The democratic spirit of the school is reflected in the absence of lines of social or financial position. No distinctions exist between the wealthiest girl or boy in school and a scholarship student. Often the latter are outstanding leaders in activities and among the most popular students in their groups. This democratic spirit is reflected by the following incidents. Last year when one of the servants of the school was dying in the hospital, his little daughter was staying with one of her classmates, the niece of the President. At the same time Rubén Batista and the son of the school gardener were working together on a committee of the Student Council. It would be difficult to say which was more popular with the class he represented.*

The observation that students from different political parties studied together without problems was certainly valid. They not only studied together; they were friends. This fact is illustrated by an action of Rubén Batista the day after his father had successfully led the coup that ousted President Prío. Rubén called Zoe Prío to be sure that she was safe and to offer his help. He did not call the niece of the man his father had deposed; he called a Ruston friend about whom he was genuinely concerned.

The Ruston scholarship policy made it possible for the son of the President of the country and Manolo Rodríguez, the gardener's son, to work on the Student Council. Many schools gave scholarships to the children of faculty members. At Ruston it included all employees of the school, regardless of their level of responsibility or remuneration. And it carried beyond this. The daughters of the employee mentioned in the *Havana Post* article continued to receive their scholarships after their father's death and both graduated from Ruston Academy.

By the time of his death in the summer of 1946, Mr. Ruston's original dream of an individual-centered school providing a college preparatory program had developed into a multi-faceted school serving a broad range of students.

One of the obituaries published in the press at the time of his death assessed his contribution as follows:

> Mr. Ruston, whose basic pedagogical philosophy was based on an unshakable faith in the "good" of every human being and the conviction that this "good" should and can only be developed by means of a liberal and generous education of the individual through close contact between students and teachers, has transformed the modest Academy of 1920 into one of the most respected institutions of private education in Cuba which presently has a student body of close to 400 students and 40 degreed teachers.
>
> This educational undertaking, which was a true contributor to understanding between all of the Americas and particularly between Cuba and the United States, received official recognition the 27th of June of 1945 on the occasion of the Silver Jubilee of Ruston Academy when Mr. Ruston was granted the Carlos Manuel de Céspedes National Medal of Honor.

FULFILLMENT OF THE DREAM
1947-1961

In his lifetime Hiram Ruston nurtured his dream school with care and sacrifice. We who followed him to take the dream to new levels built upon this strong foundation. In fact, the flowering success of this period was made possible by the combined labors of countless earlier teachers, students and parents. These years brought the fulfillment of the Ruston dream!

As Ruston grew, old goals remained unchanged. But considerable attention was given to finding better ways to implement them. Even though the student body had increased more than ten-fold, the school's chief concern was still individual students and their development. However, because the events surrounding World War II emphasized the importance of developing responsible citizens, the school focused more attention upon helping students understand that democracy was built upon citizens—upon their habits of thinking and methods of solving problems. Teachers gave increased attention to developing critical thinking and problem solving skills. Ruston became more than ever concerned about the adult-to-be.

Teaching Approaches

While continuing to emphasize the development of academic skills and the knowledge of students, all departments searched for new content and new ways to contribute to individual student growth.

Regrettably, there are only fragments of written evidence of this work. In 2000, when this history of the school is being written, only a few of the teachers could be located or were living to report what they had done.

As the Director of the Lower School, Sibyl created the plan for improving programs at this level. She worked closely with all the teachers of the Lower School to help them develop new ways to implement and enrich their programs. Unfortunately there are no detailed reports of the innovative work she did.

Sibyl worked closely with Mario Iglesias. He was responsible for designing and overseeing the Spanish program of the Intermediate Department. Both enrolled in summer study programs in American universities to assure that they were exposed to the latest educational methodologies and experiences.

Mario is one of the few teachers who produced a written record of the approaches used in Intermediate. The details of the following report reflected the new life and emphasis in all Intermediate classes.

In describing his teaching, Iglesias wrote,

> *I taught language arts and social studies in Spanish. In language teaching I emphasized the acquisition of reading and expression skills needed for communicating orally and in writing. The students were asked to read not only the readings in the textbooks but also full-length library books. Following a long Spanish tradition, we emphasized the study of grammar to serve as the normative criterion for composition.*
>
> *In social studies, the emphasis was on (1) understanding the past as a preliminary and essential step for understanding the present and the nature of the human being; (2) discovering the relations between the physical environment and the human life; and (3) using the appropriate methods for researching the past and the environment.*
>
> *Our units of study on government, the judicial system, the tropical climate, and the sugar industry were planned and conducted almost entirely by the students. The teacher acted as a facilitator of learning. We invited distinguished speakers to the classroom to present a topic to the students and answer questions from them. We went to places when seeing the real thing was better than reading about it in books.*
>
> *I tried to help the students to discover causes and relationships between apparently contradictory facts. Integration of knowledge was an important goal and the ability to express it in straight, correct oral and written language was taught and practiced in class.*
>
> *Our program was open to all kinds of innovative methodology, but the enthusiasm for the method was not the primary aim. We always kept foremost in our thinking the emotional and intellectual health of our students.*
>
> *Diversity of learning experiences: Our students were not subjected to a one-teacher experience only. On a typical school day, a student at the*

intermediate level, fourth, fifth and sixth grades, was exposed to (1) a learning experience in English, (2) another in Spanish, (3) another in Mathematics (taught in English), (4) and another in one creative or recreational activity, such as arts, sports, carpentry, sewing, puppets, music or dance. Students had the opportunity to work with at least five different teachers.

Educational philosophy: The old Ruston's educational creed was based on the concern for the student's education as a wholesome individual not only prepared to meet the challenges of the present but also the uncertainties of the future with a solid understanding of the past. We tried to help students understand that the human being lives in a historical continuum.

Reasonable quantity and quality of educational materials: Each classroom in the Lower School had a library. Spanish, as well as English classes, had their own libraries with books geared to the age level of the class. Special efforts were made to prevent inequality between books in English and Spanish.

In the High School Department similar changes were introduced as a result of the freedom provided to teachers in developing and introducing more effective teaching approaches. These "free" teachers made many valuable contributions to Ruston.

Dr. Bernard Gundlach, a refugee from Germany with a European Ph.D., taught mathematics in the Upper School. He was given classes and textbooks, but no instruction as to the methods he should use. He challenged his students by teaching them to solve problems in their heads. This habit was so strongly established with one of his students that the youth followed it to solve the problems in an important, state-administered Bachillerato examination. The public official who supervised the test refused to accept the results. He accused the student of copying the answers from a neighbor. (The evidence was clear; there were no step-by-step solutions. Only answers were given.) Knowing that the student had not cheated, we were able to convince the responsible authorities to retest the student in a totally controlled environment where only the exam monitor and the student would be in the room. Again the boy was able to provide correct answers to the test questions without doing any manual calculations. The embarrassed inspector acknowledged that he had drawn the wrong conclusion.

Gundlach was also known to utilize somewhat unusual but effective methods to get students to concentrate. One of these was to sit in a chair on top his desk and blow soap bubbles while students took his math exams.

The benefit received from the freedom granted to teachers was well reflected in the contribution Dra. Hilda Perera made to the school. I remember well the interview I had when she applied for a position. She had just graduated from the University of Havana and had no teaching experience. In fact she was not even sure that she would make a good teacher. But I saw in her potential that she had overlooked. Given freedom, she developed into a very creative teacher. Soon after she joined the staff, I needed someone to reorganize and develop the Spanish program for grades 7-12. The task was assigned to her.

Hilda's work was difficult because the students at all levels fell into two broad groups: those who had lived in Cuba many years and spoke fluent Spanish, but had little skill in writing it, and those who were just beginning. To handle this problem, she developed tests that provided the basis for dividing students into two elementary and three advanced groups with a sixth group of seniors who were preparing for the College Board Spanish Advanced Placement Examination.

The work of Senior Spanish reflected the high level of Hilda's achievement. Part of the year was devoted to studying *El Cid*, one of the most acclaimed Spanish classics, and to writing papers about the work. Since students would be required to make some translations on College Board tests, they were given practice in translating. For these exercises, Hilda used excerpts from *The Report on Cuba*, an authoritative book on the economy of Cuba and the possibilities for the country's development, written by a Special U.S. Commission that spent several years studying conditions in Cuba.

One year when the Senior Spanish class studied *La Vorágine*, Hilda suggested that the class help her write a book about this classic. The students became so excited about the project that they worked on it both inside and outside of class. The book, a collection of critical essays about the work, was later published. It received acclaim because it was a joint work of teacher and students.

Students in all of the advanced classes were required to read an additional book each month. In order to make it possible for students to meet this requirement, the school had to build up a library of books of varying difficulty. With this extra reading, students' vocabularies flourished, and they had much less difficulty expressing themselves (No English was allowed in advanced classes.)

As Hilda began her classes she quickly saw that students had special problems with gender agreement and the subjunctive forms of verbs. But these subjects were not adequately covered in textbooks. So, she wrote short practical booklets with exercises that covered these subjects. Later she combined these booklets into a single book, *Ortografía*, which has been republished ten times.

One of the basic objectives of these courses was to help students develop vocabularies comparable to that of a non-specialized, native adult. By searching books and newspapers, Hilda built up a list of words students should add to their vocabularies. Practice in the use of these words was included in *Ortografía*.

Once when asked what happened in her Spanish classes, Hilda replied, "Spanish happens!"

Another record of outstanding dedication and creativity was that of Dra. Marta Ferrer, who was in charge of the Mathematics program in High School. Her most outstanding work was with students preparing to take the College Board Mathematics Advanced Placement Examination. Marta taught at Ruston in the morning and at another school in the afternoon. After school, the College Board trainees went to her home for an additional two hours of work for which she received no remuneration. While she was giving individual assistance to one of the students, another helped entertain her two small sons.

This class met for an additional three hours of work on Saturday mornings and every day during Christmas vacation. Oh, yes, she did excuse them on December 24th and 25th and on New Year's Eve and January 1st!

I was sometimes concerned because Marta's "specialists" received grades of only B in the first months. Her tests were so difficult that no one could finish them in the time allowed. This was her way of forcing her students to work faster. Unaware of Marta's strategy, I wondered if her standards were too high. But I raised no question . . . after all I claimed that I gave teachers freedom!

Students' College Board scores showed that her "ruthless" training paid off. One year four of her students took the College Board Mathematics Advanced Placement Exam. All four had a score of 800 out of a possible 800! One of her students who later studied engineering at MIT said that he got through the first two years there on the mathematics Dra. Ferrer taught him.

The benefit of allowing teachers freedom to decide what they did was also reflected by the work of Boris Goldenberg, another European refugee with a German Ph.D. One year he found that his students in modern history knew very little about medieval history. He solved this problem by writing a summary of the earlier period which he taught before he continued with the study of the class textbook. Boris was also known to give informal lectures on philosophy and promoted informal discussions among interested students on this topic on the open porch of the main building in Vedado and, later, on the porch of the resident teachers' living area in the new building.

I participated in this creative process as well. Wearing my Coordinator of Upper School English Studies hat, I initiated a dual grading system that became notorious among the students but improved the writing of the entire Upper School. On important written work, students were given a letter grade for content of the paper and a numerical grade for mechanics. This latter grade was based on a list of penalties (different for each grade level) for errors in sentence structure, punctuation and spelling. Students who had a failing grade in mechanics at the end of the school year were required to take a summer school course to improve these skills. Failure to improve during the summer meant repeating the grade. Needless to say, most settled down and worked during the summer.

One year a girl in Senior English had a mark of minus 220 in December. The grade was a clear warning signal. The girl accepted the fact that she had to improve her technical skills. By June she had improved enough that she was allowed to participate in the graduation ceremony and receive a blank diploma. By the end of summer school she had earned her signed diploma!

The main textbook that I used in the first semester of Senior English during much of the '50s was Hayakawa's *Language in Thought and Action*. I chose this to help my students understand the important influence of language and the emotional effects that the words used had upon both the sender and receiver of a communication. Students used to talk about "what happened in Hayakawa," never about "what happened in English class." I hoped that the use of this label showed that some of Hayakawa's ideas had stuck. But sometimes I wondered if it merely reflected student reaction to my unorthodox emphasis. Later comments from students showed that Hayakawa had taken and proven valuable in their later lives.

In the Bachillerato Department, there was no way to change the content of the courses. Teachers were required to cover all of the various official programs. But in doing this, they were able to emphasize the importance of independent analysis of evidence and facts and to encourage thinking for one's self. One graduate of the Ruston Bachillerato program, who later taught at Ruston, has described her experiences as follows:

> *The courses were not limited to covering the extensive programs given by professors and members of the Ministry of Education, somehow any topic that the student encountered and was of interest deserved some class time. For example, the class was reading La Vida Es Sueño; it was noticed that Segismundo was thrown from a window to the sea, at a time when Poland had no coast line. From this point on, Geography and History were involved to locate Poland in the map and to recall the sad history of the changing borders due to war and greedy neighbors.*

Bachillerato students had seven classes a day, five to cover the official program and two in English. One of these concentrated upon developing skills in reading, speaking and writing English. The second was one in which the content of the course was taught in English. Planning English classes for this Department was difficult because students had widely varying skills in English. For example, in the second year of Bachillerato some students could take a regular ninth grade English class; some were just beginning their study of the language; and, others were somewhere in between. This problem was partially eliminated by scheduling all Bachillerato English classes in two periods. Multi-levels of work for the students of each grade were thus provided. Attention was always given to improving all class courses and to developing the skills of the individual student.

Through this multi-level approach, we were not only able to provide the level of language training which was appropriate for each student, but we also made it possible for some students to graduate with a double Bachillerato and High School degree. Those Bachillerato students who had the English qualifications to do so were able to prepare and qualify for entry into either a Cuban or American university. No other school in Cuba was able to offer such a program to their students.

Creativity and independence was a hallmark for all teachers at Ruston. Dra. Estela Agramonte supervised the Bachillerato Department and handled the challenge of doing so extremely well. She helped to create an environment where students could be well prepared to meet the qualifying exams. She created a system in which only those who could pass a pre-qualifying exam could take the public qualifying exams at the end of each academic term. Teachers shifted into a review gear several weeks before the exams were to be given to help prepare the students for their pre-qualifying run which required work on honing rote memory skills. During the remainder of the school terms, teachers were free to use more challenging techniques of education and provide the individualized stimulation synonymous with an education at Ruston Academy.

The Comercio Department program was geared to provide bi-lingual secretarial and business administration skills. Its origins and many of its main characteristics over time can be traced to the skills and dedication of Felipe de la Cruz who was associated with the program from the late 1920s until the late 1940s. The program he designed, later carried out under the direction of Mrs. Mary Suárez, was a four-year program classified as Basic, Transition, First Year and Second Year. Course work was more limited than in the other Departments but still extremely challenging. The areas covered in the program included Accounting, Basic English, Business English, Business Law, Business Math, English Grammar, Shorthand, Spanish Literature and Composition, and Typing.

Students who participated in the Comercio Department program report that their teachers were very demanding. They also report that it was extremely beneficial to them. One graduate of Comercio has written:

> *I can state categorically that had it not been for the education that I received at Ruston, my family and I would not have been able to recover and make a decent living in this country. If I had not been able to speak English, I would not have been able to help maintain my family, would not have been able to go to college, etc. But it was not only the English and the typing and shorthand skills, it was also what was inculcated in us—that we could have success in life if we worked hard, that there were no obstacles that we could not overcome, that we*

had value as individuals, and that we could take care of ourselves. And that we learned well, as can be seen, given that all of us were able to have careers and lead comfortable lives.

Extra-Curricular Activities

While focusing upon academic improvement, the school continued to emphasize extra-curricular activities. Ruston recognized the important part played in the development of a child's character by activities outside the classroom and, consequently, attempted to provide in the schedule a sufficient number and diversity of activities to enable pupils to find some activity they would enjoy. According to some students, Upper School extra-curricular activities provided the opportunity for a large proportion of the multi-cultural exchanges among them.

Arts and Crafts

In the Lower School experiences in drawing and painting were given to all children as part of the regular schedule. Sewing classes, outside the regular classes, were provided for the girls of the Intermediate. Upper School students could participate in voluntary classes in drawing and painting.

Athletics

For Lower School students, sports activities were provided in the regular schedule and also at recess and lunchtime. All older students were required to take two sport periods a week. Frequent opportunities were provided to play basketball, volleyball and baseball during and after school hours. Upper School teams for different age levels were active throughout the year for both girls and boys.

Dancing

Children began rhythmic activities in the Primary Department (kindergarten through third grade), then moved on to folk dancing when they reached the Intermediate Department (fourth through sixth grade). Girls in the Upper School (Bachillerato, Comercio and High School) were offered modern dancing. Square dancing was all the rage one year when one of the resident teachers proved to be somewhat of an expert in organizing and calling the squares.

Dramatics

Younger students were frequently given opportunities to write and produce their own plays. In the Upper School there were annual productions of well-known plays in both English and Spanish. Participating in and watching these plays gave the students knowledge of dramatic works and increased their enjoyment of the theater.

Music

The school gave considerable attention to developing students' appreciation of good music. Regular music classes in the Lower School gave all children practice in singing and in music appreciation. Music appreciation classes were also provided for Upper School students.

But most important of all were the experiences of singing with one of the school's choral groups under Sibyl's direction. There were three: the Junior Choir, the Senior Choir and the Madrigal Choir. Their most important production was the Christmas Concert, a must on the calendars of many Ruston families as well as for others in the community. I shall never forget the beautiful ending of these concerts as the lights faded while the three groups sang "Silent Night".

Being in a chorus meant hard work. In order to assure the high quality of the singing, students were admitted only on the basis of passing a voice test. One alumnus, an outstanding athlete who had studied at Ruston for twelve years, said years after graduation that he was disappointed about only one thing in Ruston—he never "made the chorus." He tried out year after year, hoping his voice had improved, but singing wasn't his forte.

This concentrated work produced exceptional music. The programs were interesting because Sibyl spent considerable time searching for new songs. I remember when she discovered "La Virgen Lava Pañales" (which roughly translates as "The Virgin Washes Diapers"). I feared that some might consider the song irreverent, but Sibyl was right. The beautiful song was an immediate, and often-repeated, favorite.

To this day Rustonians recall the impact that these Christmas concerts had upon them. These comments are frequently made by people of the Jewish faith who sang in the choir or attended all Christmas concerts. One soloist in her day commented that following one concert someone from her synagogue had approached her parents asking them why she did not sing in their synagogue as well.

Puppet Theater

The puppet theater was one of the most popular activities of the students of the fifth and sixth grades. This program which was introduced and run by Mario Iglesias gave opportunities for students to participate in the many aspects of the production: the making of the theater and costumes of the puppets, the designing and painting of the scenery, and the final production of the play.

Scout Work

Ruston was very happy to use its buildings as a scout work center for boys and girls. Though the work was not an official part of the school program, the schedule was arranged so that those who desired to participate in this program could do so easily. The school was proud of its Brownies and Girl Scouts, its Cubs and Boy Scouts.

School Dance Activities

The most popular social activity in the Upper School were the dances held several times a year. These "big nights" were school affairs attended by most of the Upper School students from Comercio, Bachillerato and High School and were organized by a student-run Dance Committee. Most Cuban mothers knew how carefully I supervised these dances and sent their daughters without chaperones. Those who continued the chaperone tradition sat in the back and enjoyed the activities. They watched the bashful younger boys gradually get up enough courage to ask a girl to dance, the teachers dancing with the girls who sat too long on the sideline, and the older students who danced for hours to the recorded orchestras producing Cuban rhythms and American rock and roll. These special evenings were a treat for all!

Movie Nights

About once a month, a movie was shown at Ruston. These activities were planned by the Movie Committee, made up of representatives from the three Upper School Departments. They chose the movie and the student operator of the projector. Usually the Committee produced a live show, a skit or musical program which preceded the movie. This was great fun!

Establishing Fundación Ruston-Baker

For the first thirty-one years, Ruston was privately-owned—for twenty-six years by Hiram and Martha Ruston, and for five years by Martha alone. In 1944, when Mr. Ruston was faced with a series of health problems, Sibyl and I returned to Havana to assist him. Shortly thereafter, papers were signed which made us owners of the school after the death of both Rustons. Mr. Ruston died in 1946; Miss Ruston in 1951.

When we inherited the school in 1951, Sibyl and I began at once to implement our plan to change the school to a non-profit foundation. We had discussed the idea of a foundation with Mr. Ruston and tried to get him to make the change before he died. But he left the school to us. He wanted us to operate it as our school during our lives. Then when we were ready to retire, if neither of our sons were interested in carrying on the school, we could set up the foundation.

But we had looked forward to this time eagerly. We never considered the school to be our private property; it was only our trust. We believed that the mission of the school was too important to depend upon two people for its continuance. We wanted Ruston to follow the plan of great private schools in the United States and England which have been able to render ever-increasing service because their legal status as non-profit foundations gave them financial security and a basis for obtaining donations from others interested in the school. It was also our hope that the work of the Fundación Ruston-Baker would demonstrate that the maximum development of educational institutions can be best achieved when the work is carried on by a group that is motivated by a sincere belief in the ideal of rendering service to the community and to the future.

The concept of a non-profit foundation was a new one for many Cubans. It took a long paragraph in the "Constitución de la Fundación Ruston-Baker" to explain non-profit foundation in Spanish. The following incident will help to illustrate this linguistic and conceptual difficulty.

One evening before we took any legal steps to form the Foundation, Sibyl and I visited Sr. Rafael Palacios, the Chairman of the school's informal Advisory Committee, to explain to him what we were going to do. The property was ours; we needed no one's approval. But as Sr. Palacios was an old friend, we wanted him to understand. What an evening!

I spent almost two hours explaining how a non-profit foundation would operate and the benefits it would bring to the school. When I thought I had at last convinced Sr. Palacios that the change would be a good one, he surprised me by his query: "But what percent of the profits do you get?" With considerable restraint I explained again: "No one gets a share in the profits, Mr. Palacios. They all go to benefit the school." Then I started my explanation again. After three hours the discussion ended. But I was never sure whether Don Rafael really understood or just stopped arguing with two foolish Americans. The basic trouble was that he had difficulty accepting the fact that two otherwise intelligent parents could be so blind to the importance of leaving an inheritance for their two sons. He had four children; it was his dream to leave a large inheritance for each of them. Despite the difference in our outlooks, Rafael Palacios was a strong and important supporter whose help would prove crucial to making our dream come true.

The Fundación Ruston Baker was formally established and registered on April 27, 1951. It was the first and only non-profit educational foundation in Cuba. The first Board was composed of the following Officers and Directors:

> Rafael Palacios, President
> Burke Hedges, Vice-President
> Mario Núñez Mesa, Secretary
> William P. Field, Treasurer
> James D. Baker, Supervisor
> William W. Caswell, Jr., Director
> Theodore Johnson, Director
> Philip Rosenberg, Director
> Elena Mederos de González, Director
> Helen H. McMasters, Director
> Herminio Portell Vila, Director

Seven of the Board members were Americans, and four were Cubans. Two of the eleven were women. Four of us were educators, three were business executives, one a lawyer, one a banker and one a public accountant.

The Board focused primarily on financial matters and left the school program and administration to me. The Directors had a clear understanding and appreciation of our respective roles in large part because many of them had previously served on the informal Advisory Committee of Ruston Academy.

For some years prior to the creation of the Advisory Committee, William Field, a public accountant and the father of a student in the '20s, had been a most valuable volunteer financial advisor to the school. Mr. Ruston concluded from this experience that it would be useful to ask others to join Mr. Field as members of an Advisory Committee that he could consult on matters where he felt that he could use assistance. This committee was created in the early '40s and functioned until the Fundación was created in 1951.

Upon the death of Mr. Ruston in 1946, I worked directly with this group in much the same way that he had. Thus the fact that the Advisory Committee members had limited themselves largely to financial matters made for a smooth transition to their Fundación roles. All on the Board realized that the major change that had taken place was a matter of ownership, which now resided not in individuals but in a non-profit foundation with a self-perpetuating Board of Directors.

Building the New Home for Ruston

Our dreams of a modern school facility started prior to the creation of the Fundación Ruston-Baker, but the creation of the Fundación was a requirement to make the dream come true. After I became Headmaster at the time of the death of Hiram Ruston in 1946, I used to retreat to the sea wall a block from the school in Vedado to escape from my worries about lack of space, lack of play areas, and crowded quarters of bedrooms-turned-to-classrooms where the normal activities of one class disturbed the class in the adjoining room. There, as I watched the waves crash against the base of the wall, I could imagine the ideal school plant I so desired. Later this vision became more concrete as I studied the plans of ideal schools portrayed in architectural magazines. Gradually this vision became a plan on paper. The architects who built the school, Gabriela Menéndez (a Ruston alumna) and her partner/husband, Nicolas Arroyo, worked closely with me to be sure that the new building would meet the special needs of Ruston.

Many of my ideas for the plan had come from a Texas architect, who was developing new concepts for a model school plant. When the plan for the new building was finally finished, this specialist was brought to Havana to see if he had any suggestions for improving our plan. After spending a day at Ruston and studying our program, the architect asked me if I knew how important the school patios were. I replied that I knew only that they were perfect reflectors of sound that created a problem for all classes. The architect then explained that the patios, which served as a student mingling center, were largely responsible for the friendly spirit he found throughout the school. He explained that, if he had to choose between sending his children to the most ideal school he had ever built or to the present Ruston with its friendly spirit, he would definitely choose Ruston, in spite of the crowded quarters.

As a result of his advice, terraces were added in our design for the new Ruston building: the large terrace beside the school office in the first wing, the large terrace at the end of the second wing where refreshments were sold at recess, and the large area outside the study hall which held two large picnic tables shaded by full-grown trees. And in the Lower School, a covered open space was left in the center of each wing to be used both as social areas and auditoriums.

Then one day while driving through the Alturas del Country Club area, I found the ideal site for our school. A realty company was developing a new residential project on a huge undeveloped section of land. Several months later, in September of 1951, the Board of Directors agreed to use the accumulated savings of the previous five years to buy nine acres of this choice land. With this act of courage, the first step toward a new home for Ruston Academy was completed!

Next came the big fundraising campaign to obtain contributions to construct the new home. When some $300,000 (about half the cost of the complete building) was raised, the Board of Directors made another wise decision. They decided to use those funds to build the super structure for the entire plant and wait until a loan could be obtained that would enable them to finish the project. For two years this bare structure of steel and concrete stood as a silent expression of our confidence in the future.

Raising funds for a non-profit foundation in Cuba was a novel experience for all of us. It was hard for some to believe that the financial resources being sought would not benefit somebody monetarily. This difficulty is well illustrated by the story of one Cuban father who served on the fundraising committee for the new building. He had visited another Cuban father to solicit a contribution. "Don't be a fool!" the other Cuban responded. "Don't you know that Baker will use that money to build an apartment house for himself!"

And indeed there were those who were convinced that our own home was built with some of these funds. We never even considered that someone might think this. Sibyl and I used our combined savings and a bank loan to build our residence across the street from the school. Because we had worked so closely with them over the years, we used the same architects who designed the school to design the house; we used the same construction company; the same color cement blocks. The costs involved in the construction of our house were totally segregated from the costs of building the school and were paid by us. And yet, there were still those who "knew" our home was built with Ruston funds. We had lived in Cuba for many years, but we still had much to learn.

The new school building was completed by faith in the Ruston dream and by the hard work that supported it. It took nine years to fulfill this dream. First, following the death of Mr. Ruston in 1946, there had been five years of waiting until the Fundación could be established. Then another delay while the fundraising campaign produced the funds to begin construction, and a last delay while a bank loan was negotiated. Finally in September, 1955, that glorious day came! Classes opened in the new building!

This accomplishment did not come easily. In late August, 1955, the school was faced with a problem. The new building was not finished, and there was no place to open classes in September. In the mad rush to finish the building on time several mothers grabbed brushes and helped to paint the Lower School classrooms. One of the construction workers was heard to exclaim, "Esas madres sí que trabajan." ("Those mothers sure can work!")

This willingness to work for Ruston was also demonstrated when the Parent Teachers' Association (PTA) volunteered to raise the money to construct the sports facilities of the new school—the volleyball courts, the basketball courts, the baseball diamonds—and to build a fence around the large sports field. To raise the $10,000 needed for this project, they planned a huge "verbena", a fair that provided many games of chance and skill, different kinds of entertainment, and a wide variety of foods. Most of the nine acres of the new plant were used for this huge party. Fathers constructed booths and managed them. Mothers prepared foods and sold them. The entire Ruston family was on hand for the celebration. And countless friends from the community came to enjoy the fun. For many Cuban parents this was a new experience. They had worked on projects to raise money for churches and charities, but never to create something for others like themselves. They experienced the satisfaction and reward of working as a group to produce something that would benefit the community of which they were a part.

Careful attention was given to the plans for landscaping the nine acres. I gave so much attention to landscaping the campus because I believed that living in a beautiful environment would contribute to students' appreciation of the beauty of nature.

Sra. Serafina Lastra de Giquel, one of the city's leading landscape architects, planned the entire project as her contribution to the school. The plants for it were grown in our Ruston "vivero" (plant nursery). Like all others connected with Ruston, this project was completed with the cooperation of many parents and friends. Mr. and Mrs. Tom Rankin, who had a house with a very large garden one block from the new school, turned a large section of their garden into a "vivero" for the school.

In Cuba plants can be easily started from cuttings. Parents saved their trimmings of choice plants for the school garden. Adelaide Buchanan Everhart, Ruston '38, and I were called the Ruston "bibijagüas" (leaf-cutter ants) because every time either of us went out into the countryside we returned with a carload of "green fragments" to be turned into large plants for the new school.

Manuel Rodríguez, the school gardener in Vedado, became the "jefe" of the new "vivero". He spent half of his time in Vedado and half at "his small farm" at the Rankin's where he worked tirelessly to grow plants and young trees.

A year or so after the gardens began to show their luxuriant beauty, a Cuban father commented to me, "The landscaping is beautiful. But the plants alone must have cost at least $10,000. Why wasn't that money used on the building?" I assured him that we had spent only about $800 on landscaping to purchase the tall palms at the entrance to the Upper and Lower Schools and the two full-grown trees that provided shade for the Upper School lunch tables outside the study hall.

A Look at the New School

Those for whom G y 5ta was "Ruston" were not prepared for the new school. It was a large four-winged building, constructed of rose-colored cement blocks. Two wings were planned for the Upper School and two for the Lower.

The first wing of the Upper School had two floors. The first floor included the school office and reception area, a faculty room, and four classrooms used for Basic English and Comercio Department classes. The second floor was headquarters for the Bachillerato Department, an office, five regular classrooms and three laboratory classrooms that were used by both Bachillerato and High School classes.

The second wing had a large room used as a study hall, library and dining room, five classrooms, as well as boys' and girls' shower rooms. One section had three floors with a garage, a workshop and a special art room at the ground level; a kitchen and rooms for the janitorial staff on the second level, and living quarters for resident teachers on the third. The four wings were joined by covered walkways.

The section for K-6 had fourteen classrooms, an office that doubled as a faculty room, and two large covered activity areas, each with a small stage at one end. The Lower School classrooms were the most unusual part of the new building. These were planned to provide for multiple activities. Each room had three sections: a spacious room for twenty-four students and a covered terrace separated by sliding glass doors, which could be opened to provide natural air conditioning or to expand the space for individualized activities. Beyond each terrace was an outdoor activity area enclosed by hedges that provided privacy for each class. Instead of walls to separate the rooms, there were specially planned dividers with individual student lockers on one side and library shelves on the other.

A recreational terrace and playground for kindergarten and pre-primary, four basketball courts (two of which were also equipped for volleyball) and two baseball diamonds were located adjacent to the spacious building.

The facilities of the new plant greatly improved the extra curricular activities, especially in sports. In Vedado we had to use the limited public facilities nearby for sports and physical education classes. Occasionally we could gain access to private facilities, but they were quite distant from the main building cluster. Here it was possible to have six games or sports activities at the same time on our own campus! The big terrace by the office could be turned into a stage much larger than the one we had at G y 5ta. The new terraces in the Lower School wings provided an ideal place for assemblies and dramatics.

We indeed had seen our dreams become a reality!

Confiscation of Ruston

The year 1959-1960, the last one the school operated its regular schedule, began well. We started with two sections of each class in grades 1-6 and a total enrollment of 750 students. In spite of the uncertainties created by Castro's "assumption of power", the school operated without serious problems. But as Castro extended his dictatorship, Ruston families, Cuban as well as American, began to move to the United States. At the opening of classes in September, 1960, there were only 150 students.

Although most Americans had left Havana by this time, Sibyl and I remained to try to save the school. We had decided that we would leave only when our Embassy left. Then on December 31st, Castro ordered our government to reduce its Embassy staff from 150 to 11. The Embassy was closed at once. Sibyl and I left for Miami four days later.

Mario Iglesias, who had been appointed Assistant Director, continued classes for the remaining Cuban students. On May 1, 1961, Ruston Academy was confiscated by the Cuban Government.

Fidel Castro took Ruston at the same time he took over all private schools in the country. At first, Ruston was called "Colegio Karl Marx". Those who had worked so hard to help create the new building were surprised to learn that the school had been built by Castro—that it was his contribution to the country. For some reason no one ever explained, the classrooms of the two wings of the Lower School were destroyed and changed into two huge storage areas. The two wings of the Upper School were kept intact. For the next forty years the Castro regime has used this part of Ruston for various programs. It is reported that the building served as an indoctrination center and a facility for feeding some of the teenagers brought to Havana from the country. They were housed in the private homes that Castro had taken over in the neighborhood. Reportedly it also served for a period of time as a sports education center for students brought into Havana from all parts of the island. In recent years the building has been in the hands of the armed forces. It is being used as a military intelligence facility and entry to it, and even photographing it, is strictly prohibited.

RUSTON'S SUCCESS

Ruston Academy judged its own success using the following standards which are found in a school brochure produced in the 1950s.

> *Each pupil who has learned here to know himself, to set his own standards on an elevated plane, and to force himself to meet those standards is, in the opinion of the school, a graduate of whom the institution may be proud. It has been and remains the policy of the school that self-discipline is the only valuable discipline, and that the guiding of pupils, as individuals rather than as groups, into the paths of self-government and self-motivation is the greatest contribution the school can make to their lives. This is the measure by which the school judges herself and by which she wishes to be judged by others.*
>
> *Ruston considers her first and most important work to be the developing of well-balanced, integrated men and women who will be responsible, active citizens in a greater democracy of tomorrow.*

We believe that Ruston was highly successful when measured by these standards.

Overall Assessment

In the '50s and early '60s, Ruston Academy had continued contact with the Inter-American Schools Service. This was the unit within the U.S. Department of State tasked to work with American schools in Latin America to assure that the children of US diplomatic, military, business and commercial personnel posted in the area had access to the best educational facilities possible. Logically we were interested in being able to meet their requirements, which at times could qualify us for small grants to help strengthen our programs. We were honored that in 1960, the Director of the Inter-American Schools Service referred to Ruston Academy as the best American school in Latin America.

Academic Achievement

Normally a school's claim to academic success is supported by students' scores on official tests. Unfortunately, these records of Ruston students were lost with the confiscation of the school in 1961. However, the following evidence shows the academic quality of the school's results.

Most of Ruston's Cuban graduates emigrated to the United States. Their outstanding success in a wide spectrum of careers in a new country reflected the quality of their education and personal development.

Evidence of the academic achievements of our students is to be found in the fact that in 1952, the children of grades 1-3 were given standardized reading tests in Spanish. The median score for each grade was more than a year and a half above that required of Cuban children of that age. (At the time, thirty-five percent of the Ruston children were foreigners for whom Spanish was a second language.)

Further indication of student accomplishment is found in the case of an American High School graduate from Ruston who knew no Spanish when he entered the school in the first grade. He had taken the College Board Spanish Advanced Placement Examination and not only qualified to receive credits towards his college degree but also fulfilled his college language requirement based upon his excellent performance on the exam. Several years after graduating this student took the United States Department of State Spanish Language Test and was rated as having Spanish language skills equivalent to those of a native Spanish speaker with a university degree. (He had clearly benefitted from the Spanish programs designed by Mario Iglesias and Hilda Perera, both of whom had taught him during his years at Ruston.)

The example above is not altogether unusual. Numerous Ruston graduates who took the College Board Spanish Advanced Placement Examination were given advanced credit in Spanish at many colleges and universities.

Most Cuban students who took College Board Entrance Examinations, which were only given in English, received scores similar to those of their American classmates.

Additional indirect evidence of the accomplishments of students is to be found in the fact that it was not unusual for High School students to transfer to such preparatory schools as Andover, Lawrenceville and Choate. There are even cases in which Cuban students taking the combined High School Bachillerato course of study were able to complete such transfers and do so very successfully.

Many of those graduating, continued their educations at leading higher education institutions, as is illustrated by the following listing of colleges and universities attended by our alumni. Because of Ruston's reputation, even some students with low grades were admitted to colleges in the United States.

Colleges Attended by Ruston Academy Alumni

Amherst College
Barnard College
Bates College
Bennington College
Boston College
Boston University
Brandeis University
California Institute of Technology
Carleton College
Carnegie Institute of Technology
Colorado School of Mines
Columbia University
Cornell University
Dartmouth College
Duke University
Georgetown University
Georgia Institute of Technology
Harvard University
Haverford College
Hiram College
Hope College
Lehigh University
Loyola College of the Université de Montreal
Macalester College
Massachusetts Institute of Technology
McGill University
Miami University
Middlebury College
Mills College
Mount Holyoke College
Mount Vernon College
New York University
Northwestern University
Oberlin College
Princeton University
Purdue University
Queens University of Charlotte
Radcliffe College
Rensselaer Politechnic Institute
Rutgers University
St. Joseph's University
San Francisco State University
Smith College
Stanford University
Stevens Institute of Technology
Swarthmore College
Syracuse University
The Citadel
Trinity College
Tufts University
Tulane University
United States Naval Academy
Universidad de La Habana
Universidad de Villanueva
University of Buffalo
University of California Los Angeles
University of Central Florida
University of Chicago
University of Florida
University of Illinois
University of Lausanne
University of Minnesota
University of Miami
University of Notre Dame
University of Oklahoma
University of Paris
University of Pennsylvania
University of Villanova
Vassar College
Wellesley College
Wharton School of Business
Yale University

Alumni Accomplishments

In evaluating Ruston's success, one asks the important question, "How successful was it as a preparatory school?"

A survey was made of the graduates of High School and Bachillerato in the classes of 1956 to 1960 to see what they had done after graduating from Ruston. The survey showed that almost all had continued their studies in U.S. colleges, the University of Havana or Villanueva University. A large number had later earned Master's degrees; many finished with a doctorate in their fields of training.

The achievement of individual Rustonians is well reflected by the example of one Cuban student, a Bachillerato student who began her studies at Ruston as a kindergartener. She went to Miami as a high school sophomore where she attended a prestigious parochial school. Shortly after her arrival, she participated in a spelling bee and became one of the finalists. She graduated as valedictorian of her class and was a top student in college, where she graduated with a B.S. in Mathematics. She received full scholarships to continue graduate studies earning a Master of Science in Mathematics as well as a Ph.D. For twenty-two years she served in several top administrative positions at the AMOCO Corporation.

The more important questions is "What contribution did the total group of graduates make?" The significance of the work of alumni could be best shown through an analysis of the contributions they made as adults. It is impossible to make such an analysis. However, the following illustrative list of some of the areas of work and positions held by some Rustonians shows the scope and importance of their work.

Positions Occupied by Alumni of Ruston Academy

Aircraft

American Airlines pilot, Texas
Coast Guard aviator, Connecticut
Director, Washington Operations, Cessna Aircraft Company, Washington, DC
Member of pilot roster serving Air Force 1 and other Presidential fleet aircraft, Washington, DC
United Airlines pilot, New York

Architecture

Partner, Arroyo y Menendez, Cuba
Partner, Maria Romañach Architects, Pennsylvania

Artists

Actress, New York
Church organist, Connecticut
Concert guitarist, Florida
Concert pianist, Virginia
Ballerina, Spain
Playwright, Washington
Jazz pianist and composer, Pennsylvania

Business

Chief Engineer, Electrowatt Engineering Consultants, Switzerland
Chief Executive Officer, American Meter Company, Pennsylvania
Chief Executive Officer, Computer Systems Software, Texas
Chief Executive Officer, Natural Microsystems, Massachusetts
Director of Manufacturing, Union Carbide Corporation, Connecticut
Director of Worldwide Business Management, Quantum Corporation, California
President, Gutierrez Company, Massachusetts
President, Lykes Brothers, Florida
Treasurer, Wendy's International, Ohio
Vice-President, PEPSICO, New York
Vice-President, The Kindrew Group, Ltd., Connecticut

Education

Assistant Principal, Belen Jesuit Preparatory School, Florida
Assistant Professor of Psychology, St. Thomas University, Florida
Associate Dean, Miami-Dade Community College, Florida
Associate Professor of Spanish, D'Youville College, New York
Associate Professor of ESL, Miami-Dade Community College, Florida
Chair, Mathematics Department, Kent Place School, New Jersey
Chairman, Department of Urban Development, University of Arizona, Arizona
Curator, Louisville Zoo, Kentucky
Dean, Colleges of Science and Technology, University of Houston, Texas
Director, Special Education Programs, North-South Center, University of Miami, Florida
Director for Bi-lingual Foreign Language Training, Dade County Public Schools, Florida
Docent, Museum of Education, Art Institute of Chicago, Illinois
Educators at the primary and secondary levels, everywhere
Ombudsman, University of Central Florida, Florida
President, Florida International University, Florida
President, Santa Monica College, California
Principal, Middle School, Texas
Professor, Department of Civil and Environmental Engineering, Duke University, North Carolina
Professor, Department of Psychology, Montclair State University, New Jersey
Professor, Spanish Department, University of Colorado, Colorado
Professor Emeritus, Foreign Languages, Gustavus Adolphus College, Minnesota
Professor of French, Amherst College, Massachusetts
Professor of Spanish, University of New Orleans, Louisiana
Professor of Spanish, Ursinus College, Pennsylvania
Senior Lecturer, Anthropology, University of Kent, United Kingdom

Financial Services

General Manager, Banco Popular Dominicano, Florida
Managing Director, J.P. Morgan and Company, New York
President, Tranter Investment Company, Ohio
President and CEO, Banco de Crédito Inversionista, Florida
President and CEO, Banco Exterior de los Andes, Florida
Senior Vice-President/Corporate Auditor, American Express, New York
Senior Vice-President/Corporate Lending, Union Planters Bank, Florida

Senior Managing Director, Bear Stearns and Company, New York

Government

Agent, FBI Counter Intelligence and Terrorism, New York
Deputy Director, Cuban Affairs, U.S. Department of State, Washington, DC
Director, Office of Latin America, U.S. Department of Commerce, Washington, DC
Foreign Service Officer, U.S. Department of State, many locations worldwide
Investment Banker, Overseas Private Investment Corporation, Washington, DC
Senior Advisor, National Institute of Health, Maryland

International Development

Chief, Environment Division, Inter-American Development Bank, Washington, DC
Chief Executive Officer, World Council of Credit Unions, Wisconsin
Executive Director, OXFAM America, Massachusetts
Field Officer, World Bank, Kenya
Vice-President, Business Development, DEVTECH Systems, Inc., Florida

Journalism

Correspondent, Time Magazine, Cuba
Director, International News Operations, CBS Television, New York
Senior Vice-President, News/Sports, UNIVISION, Florida
Vice-President, Recruiting and Talent Development, CNN, Georgia

Law

Senior Partner, Harper, Meyer & Perez, Florida

Medicine

Cardiologist, Florida
Dermatologist, Louisiana
Family practitioner, Cuba
Internist, Maryland
Professor, Division of Biochemistry, University of Texas, Texas
Professor of Anesthesiology, University of Florida, Florida

Professor of Dentistry, University of Florida, Florida
Professor of Pre-natal Surgery, Florida Institute of Diagnosis and Therapy, Florida
Professor of Vascular Surgery, University of California Los Angeles, California

Publishing

Director of Travel Publishing, National Geographic Society, Washington, DC

Religious

Bishop, Diocese of South Carolina, Episcopal Church, South Carolina
Brother, Mount Savior Monastery, New York
Minister, Episcopal Church, California
Minister, United Church of Christ, Massachusetts

Research

Assistant Director, Cuban Research Institute, Florida International University, Florida
Director, Research Center for Language and Culture, University of Texas, Texas
Meningitis B Biomedical Research Team, Cuba

Other

Corporate Controller/Chief Financial Officer, Goodwill Industries, California
Interpreters, United Nations and other similar organizations
Manager of Disaster Logistics, American Red Cross, Washington, DC

FACTORS CONTRIBUTING TO RUSTON'S SUCCESS

The evidence of the achievements of Ruston alumni raises the questions: What produced this success? What made Ruston unique?

When Ruston's physical equipment prior to 1955 was compared with that of important private schools in the States, the school was far from special. It lacked the large library, the well-equipped laboratories, the wealth of teaching aids that could so enrich class work at that time. It had no endowment, no outside source of income (except for the one time contributions to the new building). It was operated solely with the income from tuition.

It was the complexity of the colored threads in its tapestry that made Ruston unique. Some were academic; others were created by the individual relationships established by its members.

- Ruston was truly a bi-lingual school.

  All students at all levels were required to study both Spanish and English. But, one might add, most good schools require students to study at least one other language. In Ruston it was not a matter of "studying" another language. All students did concentrated work in speaking, reading, and writing both languages. All students who graduated from a department in the Upper School were fluent in a second language.

- Multiple levels of work were provided in both languages.

  This dual program began in fourth grade and was continued in all levels and all departments of Upper School. This allowed us to provide appropriate levels of language instruction in both English and Spanish to all students in the Bachillerato, Comercio and High School Departments. It is a clear example of the creativity of teachers at Ruston Academy.

- Ruston created a multi-cultural environment.

  The blend of American and Cuban culture was reflected in all phases of school life. An appreciation of the cultures of different countries was developed in history classes in both Lower and Upper Schools. The presence of children from ten to twenty countries added a one-on-one meaning to cultural diversity. Ruston provided an environment in which the children of Cubans, Americans, Asians, and Europeans—Protestants, Catholics and Jews—the children of business persons, professionals and diplomats—worked and played together as friends.

- High academic standards were maintained throughout the school.

  Mastery of skills was required at all levels in all departments. Students were challenged with difficult tasks that required hard work. Teachers gave assignments that developed a student's abilities to evaluate ideas and to search for solutions to problems. Class work required students to seek the facts in different situations, to relate the past to the present, the present to the future. Teachers helped students understand that quality results in any area can be produced only by careful, thorough work

- Ruston maintained small classes at all levels.

  Enrollment in all classes was limited to twenty-four students. The school believed that individual attention to students—to their development of skills and values—is possible only when teachers work with small groups. This advantage was guaranteed by rigid admission policies—when a class had twenty-four, no more were admitted. Often the school was unable to accept all the children in a family. Those siblings for whom there were no spaces were put on a select waiting list. Usually vacancies for them developed the following year. When parents objected to having their children in different schools, I explained that Ruston Academy could guarantee quality education for those accepted only by limiting enrollment. This importance placed upon small classes was reflected by the fact that when we planned the elementary classrooms of the new building, there was space for only twenty-four children's lockers in each.

- Teachers were given freedom to create and to act.

   This policy of giving teachers considerable freedom was not only an evidence of the school's confidence in them; it was also a challenge. Being given freedom to develop their own ways increased teachers' self-confidence and encouraged them to work hard. The first success they produced caused them to continue to search for better methods and to give more to their work.

- Teachers were partners with the administrators.

   Ruston was a cooperative creation of administrators and teachers. The close relations between the two groups produced a dynamic team that worked together as equals (freely discussing ideas and at times disagreeing about policies, strategies and programs). Administrators encouraged teachers to be creative and supported them in initiating new programs and projects.

- All administrators were teachers.

   The relationship between administrators and teachers was strengthened by the fact that all administrators were either full-time or part-time teachers. The administrators experienced teachers' problems first-hand. Some administrators wore several hats. Sibyl was Director of the Lower School, Coordinator of all English studies in the Lower School, Director of Ruston's three choral groups and full-time teacher of sixth grade English and Social Studies. Dr. Mario Iglesias was Assistant Director of the Lower School, Coordinator of Spanish studies in the Intermediate Department and full-time teacher of sixth grade Spanish and Social Studies. Dra. Estela Agramonte was director of the Bachillerato Department and part-time teacher of Spanish literature. Felipe de la Cruz and Mary Suárez ran the Comercio Department and also taught full-time in this program. I was Headmaster of Ruston, Coordinator of Upper School English and teacher of Senior English.

   Yes, even "the boss" taught! I insisted upon keeping Senior English even when supervising the building of the new school took me away from school frequently. (I once explained that I was willing to be office boy most of the day, but I wanted to enjoy at least one of the hours.)

- There were close relations between teachers and students.

  The close and friendly relations between teachers and students colored all aspects of school life. Students sensed and responded to the deep caring that was the foundation of these relationships. By helping students appreciate their potential and get to know who they were, the teachers stimulated in students the kind of self-confidence that is essential to the development of strong individuals. Students were encouraged to set high standards for themselves and to discipline themselves to meet those standards. By expecting much of students, teachers led them to expect much of themselves.

  Monthly department faculty meetings, at which the work of each individual was discussed, contributed to a better understanding of students' problems. Each teacher was aided by constructive input from others who had worked with the same students previously or were teaching them other subjects at the same time.

- Emphasis was placed upon self-discipline.

  Paramount in the program for individual growth was an emphasis upon self-discipline. In Ruston there were few discipline problems. The school made clear the norm of behavior it expected from students. We tried to help boys and girls understand the reason for certain procedures and to influence them to want to cooperate in a practice that was for the best interest of the group. And the students lived up to the expectations. Students knew they had certain liberties and rights and exercised them with responsibility. Because appropriate behavior was expected, disruptive behavior rarely occurred.

- Teachers were dedicated workers.

  Ruston teachers worked long hours at home, planning their work—not because they were loaded down with tasks from the office, but because they were caught up in the common goal of finding better ways to motivate their students.

  When talking to teachers applying for a position, I often explained that I could not offer them a high-paying job. I also told them that they would probably work harder than they ever had before. The closer was an assurance that they would have the very special reward of knowing they had made a significant contribution to the development of their students.

- Teachers cooperated very closely with the school.

    Because they were given unusual freedom, teachers felt that Ruston was *their* school. They willingly cooperated in every way they could. This contributed to unusual faculty continuity at the school. They made vital contributions at all stages of the development of the school.

- In Ruston there was an all-pervading spirit of friendliness.

    This spirit of friendliness was felt any time students met in classrooms, in patios, on the sports field, as students gathered around the snack bar at recess or at the lunch tables at noon, on trips and picnics—students from many countries were united by a single bond—they were all Rustonians.

- Ruston environment produced mutual understanding and tolerance.

    This environment didn't just happen. It was produced by Ruston philosophy, values, goals and policies. By placing emphasis upon these, the school created the happy, friendly atmosphere in which children concentrated upon being good Rustonians and forgot their differences. Teachers took advantage of every opportunity to cultivate understanding, appreciation and respect for the culture and values of different countries. There was no place in Ruston for discussing politics and sectarian religion. Working, studying, playing together, children forgot their differences and remembered only that they were friends.

    Students were encouraged to try to understand the problems of their classmates and to help them reduce these difficulties. Teachers used this group spirit as a basis for instilling the adult values of serving the community and working to help develop a better world.

- Parents worked for Ruston.

    The school worked closely with parents in guiding and stimulating the growth of each child. Meetings with individual parents contributed to a mutual understanding of a child's problems and his or her potential. These meetings helped to find solutions for the former and to encourage the latter. They also contributed donations, volunteered for special school activities, and even put paint brushes to use when needed.

- Ruston concentrated upon developing adults who will work for the community and contribute to the future.

  This end could be achieved only by influencing the goals students set for their adult lives, by creating in them the desire to become productive contributors. In history and social science classes, teachers presented an indirect challenge by emphasizing the way individual leaders influenced events in their communities and in a nation. They explained the need for dedicated leaders who can help find solutions for today's complex problems.

- Students accepted the challenge.

  The factors listed above that made Ruston Academy unique played a vital part in producing Ruston's success. But they worked only because the students wanted to become the kind of adults that Ruston strove to develop. They believed in the dream and were willing to work hard to meet Ruston's challenge.

  The students became partners in this process. They were given academic freedom. They were encouraged to search for facts to support their own conclusions in their study of material, to think for themselves. They moved toward the goal to become self-directed adults who were controlled by self-discipline and guided by their own values.

Faith as the Primary Factor

All of the factors listed above were important contributors to the success of Ruston Academy. But there is one final overriding factor which merits separate treatment given that none of the others could have come into play had it not been for faith.

The continued commitment, the tenacity, the dedication of those who made Ruston a success were all driven by one factor—faith that these dreams could be turned into reality—faith that these dreams could produce adult achievers. Ruston and her success were created by many dedicated workers who were empowered by this.

Many schools strove to produce highly developed, skilled, trained minds. But Ruston was also concerned about the *quality* of the individual students and the contribution they would make as adults. This was an ideal all could work for. Their faith would support them as they labored to create this ideal. This evidence of faith in dreams is found throughout the Ruston story.

It began with two Americans whose faith was so strong that it led them to a new country to invest their life savings and more than twenty-five years of tireless labor in a project to create a new kind of school, dedicated to achieving untested goals. It was faith that in 1951 caused the Fundación Ruston-Baker Board to invest the total accumulated savings of the school in nine acres of land. This same faith led the Board to construct the superstructure for the new building without any assurance they would be able to obtain a loan to complete the work. It was the strong, unwavering faith in Ruston's contribution to the future that led Sibyl and me to spend nine years planning and working for the new building. And it was what motivated hundreds of students, teachers, alumni, parents and friends to cooperate in building a new home for the school.

The construction of our new building showed students that by working together a group of dedicated people can produce miracles. When it was first discussed, many people had called the new building an unachievable dream. Not only did the students know the satisfaction that comes from producing a benefit for the community, they also knew that dreams can be turned into realities. They could, therefore, understand the reward they could receive as adults working to help create a better community, a better future.

Understanding the crucial role that faith played in creating Old Ruston will help all involved in working for a new Ruston. Knowing this power of faith will help them as they work to reverse the destruction of Castro's communism and develop a new Cuba.

OLD RUSTON GAVE LIFE TO DREAMS OF THE PAST. IN NEW RUSTON THERE WILL BE NEW DREAMERS TO TURN THEIR VISIONS INTO BETTER WAYS OF ACHIEVING RUSTON'S GOALS.

PART TWO

TOWARD CREATING A NEW RUSTON FOR THE FUTURE

LATEST CHAPTER OF THE RUSTON STORY 1961-2000

The success of Ruston Academy which came about as a result of dedication, a team effort and faith that dreams could come true came to an abrupt halt in May of 1961, when the school was expropriated by the Castro government. And yet, the spirit lives on.

Alumni Activities

One has only to attend a Ruston reunion to know how alive the Ruston spirit is today. To hear the shouts as old friends meet again. To share the "abrazos fuertes" (big hugs). To watch teenagers-turned-grandparents swaying to Cuban rhythms or swinging in a Conga line. Each of the reunions has been attended by several hundred Rustonians and their spouses, teachers, parents and friends. They have been such joy-filled days that many alumni have returned again and again. Those who missed the fun one time planned carefully to make the next reunion. They have been weekend affairs with a cocktail party on Friday night, a business meeting on Saturday morning, and the big dinner dance on Saturday evening. These festive reunions have been living proof of what Ruston meant to her students!

There have been seven reunions. The first was held in July, 1975, the latest in July, 2000. Because of the large numbers of Rustonians in South Florida, all of these celebrations have been held in Miami. Margarita Oteiza Castro '51 initiated the first celebration. Rocky Harper '60 and Celia Suárez '60 with the help of a committee planned and promoted the second. John Motion and his committee were the hard workers behind the next three. John organized a Ruston support group called Friends of Ruston. He printed the first Ruston directory which gave the names and addresses of over 250 former students, teachers and parent supporters. This effort led to the establishment of a computerized database which is used as the source of our mailing list. Today this database contains more than 3,500 names and the addresses for approximately 1,000 of them.

The last two reunions have been organized by the Ruston-Baker Educational Institution (RBEI) with major assistance from Ben Recarey, Margarita Oteiza Castro, Olga Cano, Celia Suárez, and Sergio Megías.

In addition to these big reunions, there have been numerous Christmas parties in Miami. Other alumni groups in California, New Mexico, and Washington, D.C. have organized regional get-togethers. These mini-reunions have shown that the Ruston spirit is still alive and strong! The faith in the Ruston dream reflected at these celebrations can be a vital force in helping to create a new Ruston for the future.

This living Ruston spirit led Bob Allen '46 to create a Ruston Academy web page in 1996. It can be found at *WWW.RUSTONACADEMY.ORG*. Bob started this site as a means of trying to locate old friends from the period when he had been at Ruston as a boarding student. He kindly agreed to expand the site to make it readily accessible to all those interested in the school.

Over the years Chris Baker has carried out several other important keep-the-spirit-alive projects. His first effort involved collecting copies of the yearbooks published by the school. This was a very difficult task given that most Rustonians had to leave their yearbook collections behind when they left Cuba. His research determined that the first yearbook was published in 1940, and the editor was Marvin Shapiro, the very same man who fifteen years later would be responsible for creating much of the furniture and built-in lockers which characterized the hallways of the Upper School and the classrooms of the Lower School in the new building. The last yearbook was published in 1960. Chris was able to locate all but one of the editions which were then used to produce photocopied versions of the yearbooks. They were also used to reconstruct a listing of the students and faculty of Ruston Academy between 1940 and 1961. He is today in the process of carrying out a new project, this time to scan all of the yearbooks so that they can be made available on compact discs (CDs) easily viewed on most computer screens.

THE RUSTON-BAKER EDUCATIONAL INSTITUTION (RBEI)

The collapse of the Soviet Union in 1999 opened a new window of hope. It looked as if Castro's days of control would soon end. Over the years we had kept the Board of the Fundación Ruston-Baker alive. Elections for new Board members were held periodically to fill vacated positions. Thus it was that I was able to hold a meeting of the Board of Directors in 1990 to start the challenging job of initiating a strategy that would lead to the re-opening of Ruston Academy as soon as the Castro government fell. Additional Board members were elected and work was initiated.

Between 1990 and 1992 the Board of the Fundación researched and developed tentative plans to launch the school once again. We looked at curriculum issues, physical plant and logistical questions, even ran three different budget projections based upon different operational assumptions. We talked about the importance of being able to recover the buildings that had been expropriated. And we also talked about the need for a new Ruston to assure Cuban student enrollment through a scholarship program and to provide evening and week-end adult education programs. We talked about a center for democratic studies and a center for the study and application of computer technology in education. We met with U.S. State Department staff from the Cuba Desk and with Agency for International Development staff responsible for the support of American overseas schools. We held discussions with Florida International University on the possibility of carrying out joint efforts in Cuba. There was no scarcity of ideas, initial inquiries and discussions.

As had been done prior to 1990, we held business meetings at each one of our Ruston Reunions and shared what we were thinking, exploring and doing with those in attendance.

But the changes that we had thought would come to Cuba did not materialize. And we realized that we could not predict when or how things would change. As Margarita Oteiza Castro put it in discussing an effort to draw up a proposed curriculum, "We have five blind people who are not only trying to describe an elephant; they are also trying to choose the type of suit that it will need."

Clearly we could not go any further in our efforts to develop concrete plans for a return to Cuba. None of us had been back to Cuba. We were stabbing in the dark. And this conclusion led the Board of the Fundación to two conclusions.

The first conclusion was that, rather than trying to focus on detailed operational plans, we should focus on maintaining and improving the Ruston network. And the second conclusion was that we should focus upon the establishment of an institution which could respond to the fundraising needs that would arise when the opportunity to return to Cuba materialized.

The first conclusion led us to commit to the continuation of the types of events and activities which would help to keep the Ruston family together. The second conclusion led to the creation of a duly registered foundation in the United States which would be in a position to carry out the desired fundraising.

Following appropriate research and the development of the by-laws needed to establish a foundation, the Ruston-Baker Educational Institution (RBEI) was registered in the State of Florida in March of 1992. Its objectives are to "research, investigate and promote the establishment, organization and maintenance of a bi-lingual school in Cuba that reflects, to the extent possible, the ideals and objectives evidenced by Ruston Academy."

The most important work of the RBEI Board has been that of defining the goals of the organization. It has also worked to locate "lost" Rustonians and to increase contacts with all members of the Ruston family. It has printed periodic newsletters, planned and directed two reunions and published a Ruston Academy Directory at the time of each of the past three reunions.

IRS certification of the organization as a duly recognized tax-free organization came in 1994 thanks to the efforts of Lawrence Ploucha, Esq. of Paul, Landy, Beiley & Harper, P.A. Mr. Ploucha was a colleague of Ruston graduate George Harper and provided this assistance on a pro-bono basis. The certification permits donors to report contributions to RBEI as tax-deductible items.

Initial fundraising efforts focused upon establishing a Believers' Fund in 1997. Rustonian donations to this fund exceed $25,000. The fund will be used to finance initial RBEI exploratory activities when conditions in Cuba justify the work that will be required to develop a realistic plan to re-open our school in Havana.

The next stage in the development of the work of the RBEI Board was that of beginning to identify what types of materials were needed to tell our story effectively and to define the purpose of the fundraising that we would initiate when the proper circumstances arose. And this led us to concentrate on a series of exercises to define the Mission and Goals of RBEI and a Ruston Academy for the future.

The Directors who have served on the RBEI Board are:

Christopher Baker
James D. Baker
Mariada Bourgin
Kenneth Campbell
Olga Cano
Kenneth Crosby
George Harper
Stuart Lippe
Modesto Maidíque
Carlos Molina
John Motion
Clarence Moore
Leo Núñez
Siomara Olano
Margarita Oteiza Castro
Ben Recarey
Ricardo Sánchez
Celia Suárez
Julio Ulloa

MISSION AND GOALS OF A RUSTON ACADEMY FOR THE FUTURE

The Mission and Goal Satements of RBEI are statements which have been formally adopted by our Board. They are the result of initial work done by the Board, which was then distributed to former faculty and students, and finalized by the Board after completing a review of the commentary and suggestions of these Rustonians. Like all planning outcomes, ours needs to be viewed as a work in progress. The mission and goals adopted by RBEI are as follows.

RBEI Mission Statement

The Ruston-Baker Educational Institution will perpetuate the Ruston Academy vision and legacy by promoting activities that reflect the values, educational objectives and philosophy reflected by its goals. It will also continue to strive towards the re-establishment of Ruston Academy in the free and democratic Cuba of the future.

RBEI Goals—Contributions to Students

- Ruston Academy will strive to guide the personal and academic growth of students by helping them develop self-knowledge, critical thinking skills and tolerance in ways that will prepare them to be productive, participating citizens, capable of helping create a better future.
- Ruston Academy will promote cultural understanding among students of all nations by providing a multi-cultural educational environment in small class settings that will encourage close personal relations. To this goal a special scholarship will be established to assure the greatest possible enrollment of Cuban students in the early stages of re-opening.

- Ruston will concentrate on providing a solid background of knowledge which will emphasize the most recent advances in science and technology as well as a liberal arts education. Students will be expected to acquire mastery of academic skills while developing good work habits. Students will develop the ability to evaluate ideas and search for answers in order to produce independent thinkers. Students will be encouraged to strive for academic excellence. Hopefully, after graduation, Ruston alumni will continue a life-long pursuit of knowledge and culture.
- Ruston Academy will give major attention to understanding students' strengths and weaknesses by guiding them to overcome their weaknesses and to develop their strengths and special skills to their fullest potential. To this end, Ruston will provide an environment of mutual respect and freedom that will stimulate personal growth and inner discipline.
- Ruston Academy will provide extracurricular activities in the areas of sport, technology and the arts. These pursuits will help produce well-rounded individuals with multiple interests and capacity for enjoyment.
- Ruston will provide students with an environment where the conduct of all participants will reflect democratic values and principles as well as the highest ethical standards.

RBEI Goals—Contributions to Cuba

- Ruston Academy will place great emphasis on all areas that will contribute to the future of Cuba. Through education, it will support and promote the strengthening of the civil society, economic development and democratic principles.
- Ruston will provide an elementary through secondary program in both English and Spanish that will graduate fully bi-lingual students capable of entering institutions of higher learning in both Cuba and abroad.
- Ruston will provide a Business Administration Department that will graduate bi-lingual students with the technical knowledge and skills that will enable them to work in both Cuban or foreign corporations and other entities requiring trained personnel.
- Ruston will provide a Center of Adult Education to meet the needs of the community in the areas of computer technology as well as in learning to speak, read and write in English.
- Ruston will serve as a demonstration center which Cuban and foreign educators will use as a forum to discuss new academic methods and new technologies that will help stimulate student growth. The school facilities will be made available for seminars for Cuban and foreign educators.

WHAT NEXT?

Feasibility Studies

Though frustrating, the last fifteen years have been productive. Those who have been involved in the exercises to define a future Ruston have initiated a process for the re-opening of our school in Havana. But much of the work that we have done lacks an informed perspective. Before going much further, it is essential that we know more about Cuba and the educational challenges it will be facing.

We must be ready to initiate on the ground feasibility studies as soon as the opportunity to do so arises. And we must continue to mobilize the funds that will be needed in order to carry out such studies.

Recovery of Property

We need to be in a position to move rapidly, at many levels, and effectively to assure that the school building and grounds owned by the Fundación Ruston-Baker are returned to us. Any attempt to pursue the goals which we have set for ourselves will be immensely more difficult if we fail to attain use of our buildings as a first step to re-establish a presence in Cuba.

Interim Measures

Over the years a number of alumni involved in education have suggested to me that it would be useful to know more about the Ruston Academy model. They have expressed an interest in learning more about the methods which were used at Ruston; they would like to see if there are any ideas that could be applied in other school settings.

Hopefully this book will provide at least part of what was being sought. To the extent that we can, we ought to find ways we can share our experiences with others equally committed to the concept of student-centered education.

This then is the noble history of Ruston Academy. The Ruston which influenced so many in profound ways was the creation of countless dreamers who believed in an ideal and labored ceaselessly to turn their dreams into reality. A Ruston for the future which will perpetuate these values, goals and spirit, must be produced by the same process. Today we strive to understand the forces that guided past actions in order to better emulate the example of past creators. The achievements of the past are our challenge for the future!

As I end this history of Ruston Academy, my mind turns to a future assembly of the Intermediate Department in our old school in Alturas del Country Club in which we can all join the students as they proudly sing a slightly modified version of our school song.

>**Ruston forever! Her fame will never die!**
>**We'll fight for her colors, and raise them up on high**
>**Strong are the bonds of our love and loyalty**
>**Making the future what we want it to be**

PART THREE

MEMORIES

RUSTON IN THE WORDS OF OTHERS

Ruston Academy was different things to different people. This posthumous section of the book brings together a selection of the documents left by James D. Baker at the time of his death. In these we find a wealth of information that helps to round out this history of Ruston Academy. Hopefully it will provide the reader with a better understanding of what Dad has referred to as "the complexity of the colored threads in its tapestry that made Ruston unique".

We start this section with a most unique reflection from a special guest to Ruston Academy in July of 1959. This month marked the arrival in Havana of a large number of people from the interior of the country who came to Havana to participate in a farmers' march on the occasion of the 26th of July celebration held that year. Thousands of humble, country people or "guajiros" descended upon the city and a call was put out to help lodge and feed these visitors. Ruston responded and put up a group for a number of days. And in this group there was a poet of sorts, who prior to leaving wrote down the following "décimas" (poem/song with ten lines per verse) on a blackboard in the class room where he and others had been sleeping. How appropriate that simple rhyme was his chosen way of saying a sincere thank you to a school whose motto was "only poets know the real truth"!

Close examination of the first two décimas raises questions as to whether both were written by the same person. Both appeared in an issue of the school newspaper which identify both as the product of one person. I would have to assume that the first was written with some grammatical assistance and the second was not.

Chris Baker

Francisco Lorenzo Díaz
July 1959

AL RUSTON

Guajiro, las atenciones
que nos dan en esta casa
el límite sobrepasan
de las consideraciones
Son tantas las emociones
que sentí en este lugar,
que nunca podré olvidar
al amigo cocinero
al chofer, un caballero
que nos conduce a pasear.

Este colegio es tan bello
y de tal arquitectura,
que nunca en mi agricultura
logré imaginar aquello.
Mucho supe de atropello
en la era batistiana,
de la tortura inhumana;
pero jamás de placer
ni que iría a recorrer
tantas casas en La Habana.

Adiós Habana querida;
ojalá te vuelva a ver;
me voy con el padecer
que deja la despedida.
Necesaria es la partida,
porque me espera en Placetas,
inquieta entre las inquietas
una mujer y un bebe,
una mujer y un bebe,
que con amor besaré

A TODOS LOS AMIGOS DE ROSTON ACADEMIA

Si bassa la Habana un día
bes a Roston Academia
donde un perzonal te premia
con sincera cortesía
yo jamás olvidaría
aquellos días de placer
a la Mices Aren Ver
Simpática y complaciente
es la mujer más desente
que en el mundo puede haber.

Mister Beker que decensia
se descubría en su charla
que jamás podré arrancarla
del disco de la consiencia
Todo fue paz y prudencia
en aquel resinto urvano
y el campesino Cubano
se trajo buena impreción
del trato y la educación
del Mister Americano

De la Doctora Agramonte
de sus dos hijos decentes
tan nobles y consecuentes
con los Guajiros del monte
Le pido trino al sinsonte
para cantarles a ellos
y busco argumentos bellos
nacidos en la pradera
Robándole a la palmera
esmeraldinos destellos.

*Chacha y Osmilda nos dieron
Pruebas de filantropía
Meri, con su simpatía,
que dichosos nos hicieron
EL día que nos dijeron
que debíamos partir
cuanto tube que sufrir
aquello fue como un sueño
pintoresco y alagüeño
que no podía Proceguir.*

*Los Choferes, que perzonas
de más calma y de más tino
Un trato alegre y divino
más de lo que tu ambisionas
te aturdes, y te emosionas
ante tantas atenciones
y si en mis demarcaciones
bienen un dia visitarme
juro que ban a encontrarme
fiel a sus disposiciones*

*A Uilian el culinario
que hace un perfecto potaje
también su recuerdo traje
y lo estory mentando a diario
Lo mismo le digo a Mario
que tanta lucha le dimos
y su trato rcsibimos
sin demostrarnos rencor
pues nos trato este señor
como no lo merecimos.*

MUCHAS GRACIAS A TODOS

Some years later a student, who had been at Ruston at the time that the "guajiro décima" was written, would express his own feelings and recollections in the same Cuban "décima" form.

Pedro Saavedra
Class of 1963

DECIMAS RUSTONIANAS

Allá donde Julio Pita
se dedicaba a otra cosa
y a González Espinosa
le llamaban "Bijirita"...
Donde el "hamburger" fue "frita"
y "Albóndiga" un profesor,
fue que yo tuve el valor
de escribir una cuarteta
tildándome de poeta
sin merecer el honor.

De hacer alardes me guardo
ni en el orgullo me inmerso
que en Ruston no hubo verso
como aquellos de Abelardo.
No pretendo ser un bardo
con el calibre de Uva,
mas permítanme que suba
para sacarle a mi lira
una décima guajira
que me recuerde a mi Cuba

Allá no había Internet
para enterarse de todo,
y así que el único modo
era por Coky Mallet.
Yo era vate de carnet
y hasta los chismes rimaba;
por eso es que bromeaba
que si la musa me anima
tiendo a merendar con rima
los casquitos de guayaba.

Tú sabes, pues no eres necio,
que yo sé lo que tú aprecias
los nombres de Mario Iglesias
y Alicia González-Recio.
Mas ¿cómo ponerle precio
a la entrañable tutela
que la Doctora Varela
proporcionó con fervor
provocándome este amor
por la décima espinela?

Y es que aquella escuela mía
de mi saber fue una fuente
que allí paulatinamente
aprendí geografía.
Desde la cafetería
cerca de la biblioteca
se escucha una voz que peca
más por sonora que fina,
y era la Señora Nina
pregonando su "¡Jaqueca!"

Por allá no corre el Duero
ni se decía "Vos sois";
allí había el "Hello boys!"
de Don Jaime el Panadero.
Fue allí el lugar al que quiero
decir sólo un "hasta luego",
fue el lugar al que me niego
decir permanente adiós—
donde conocí a esos dos...
a Serapio y al Gallego.

Tellaeche daba el arte
y Alonso, carpintería.
La flota la dirigía
el regimiento de Ugarte.
Ese era un lugar aparte
de la sabana o del monte,
y allí cantaba el sinsonte
unas veces su canción
y en otras su imitación
de la Doctora Agramonte.

*Y yo pasaba más rato
por tres años más un tercio
con la chicas del Comercio
que las del Bachillerato.
¿Y quién olvida a Ester Tato,
que fue nuestra actriz premiada,
en fingir tan agraciada
que pienso que es maravilla
que nunca fue fierecilla
ni mucho menos domada?*

*Y en vez de cantar el Credo
de cantar tengo memoria
aquel himno de que Oria
se había cortado un dedo.
Por recordar no me quedo
por no quedárseme nada
y recuerdo como a cada
oportunidad votamos
por Silvia, a la que nombramos
como más sofisticada.*

*Diez décimas hago, y Diez
era nuestro compañero.
A diez he llegado y quiero
terminar por esta vez.
De Ulloa he de hablar después,
y de Sergio con placer,
de Gustavo Mustelier,
de Joaquín, y de Raúl
y de nuestro cielo azul
que ayer me viera nacer.*

Hiram H. Ruston

Letter Sent to Father of
Victoria Cueva
Class of 1937

January 7, 1937

Dear Mr. Cueva:

Thank you very much for your check of January 4 for $181.35 in payment of Victoria's tuition from January to June.

You are certainly one of our best and promptest patrons and Victoria continues to be one of our best pupils. We can not expect more!

Victoria certainly is phenomenal. How she carries so many subjects and gets such excellent notes amazes me. All this in addition to the time she puts on music. You should have been to our Christmas play. Victoria did wonderfully. She has a very beautiful voice—one that she can develop professionally if she cares to do so. But, that is characteristic of her: everything she touches, she glorifies.

With best wishes for the new year, I remain,

Very sincerely yours,
H. H. Ruston

Max Healey Ruston
English and History Teacher, 1936-1940
Ruston Yearbook 1940

THE AIM OF EDUCATION

As the graduates of the Senior Class of 1940 hopefully approach the solemn night which heralds their entrance into a new and larger world, most of them will, no doubt, have vague wonderings about this whole matter of education. What is it? What should it achieve? Where does it lead? I do not propose to answer here and now a question which has perplexed every philosopher from Plato down to the present day. I do propose, however, to state what seems to me to be the marks of an educated man and what I believe education should achieve for one.

If I were asked to give in a single word a definition of education, that word would be Tolerance. For it seems to me that Tolerance, a recognition of the rights of others, an appreciation of their feelings, their beliefs, and their innermost convictions, no matter how widely divergent from our own, is more than any other thing the true stamp of an educated individual. Certain things are not conducive to Tolerance. War, more quickly than any other circumstance in environment, can narrow us, cramp us, limit us in dangerous ways. War psychosis is a disease from which the healthiest minds rarely recover once they have succumbed to it. Therefore, in such times as these, it is more important than ever before that in our effort to combat certain forces that we not adopt the very tactics which made those forces obnoxious to us at first. Yet this is done daily. If ever we wish to establish the superiority of our ideals and our way of life over and above another way of life, it must be by facing it in open, honest competition, not by adopting the very methods we so strongly deprecate in our opponents.

Present day civilization seems founded on principles not unlike those embodied in the following brief parable. A Christian and a Mohammedan were once arguing heatedly about the relative values of their professed faiths. Exasperated after more than an hour of futile argument, the Mohammedan snatched up a brick-bat, laid it solidly against the Christian's cranium, and thereby indisputably proved the superiority of the Moslem faith over Christianity! How much better had each of the disputants illustrated his arguments by works more harmonious with the faith he advocated. This is what we may call gaining a point without proving it; figuratively, it is shouting down our opponent. The difficulty with settling major issues in this way is that they are never really settled, but only suspended until our adversary has had time to refurbish his arms and accomplish a return to fighting parity with us. When this is achieved the process begins anew. Yet all too many disputes are settled on this basis. It is precisely this sort of proof we are invoking when we contend that So-and-so College is the better institution of learning because it has the better football team!

No less a sage than George Bernard Shaw has said, "Though all society is founded on intolerance, society has improved only through tolerance". I would say that "man in society" has improved only through tolerance. Thus, graduates of 1940, remember that each act of tolerance on your part is a milestone along the endless road of education. Remember that each act of intolerance indicates only the extent to which you are uneducated.

Ted Heilman
Class of 1941

An enjoyable memory which I have is of the recesses and walking the few blocks down to the Malecón with Dr. Alvarado shepherding us down there for some fresh air. Many times the waves were thundering over the sea wall and we would play chicken with them, frequently getting a little wet in the process. Then came Dr. Alvarado's loud "Vaaaaaamooos" and we knew recess was over and it was time to return to classes.

RUSTON ALUMNI ASSOCIATION NEWLETTER
December, 1942

At this time of the year we always begin to wonder how the school is shaping up in the new term. In order to get a good picture of the activities and personalities at the beginning of Ruston's 23rd year, we have asked Ted Viaux to write us a few lines on the subject.

Ruston 1942-1943

Ruston's 1942-1943 season opened to an excellent start with a total enrollment of about 285 students and an enlarged boarding department of 24 students.

Due to the gasoline shortage we were forced to change our time schedule as it was impossible for our distant patrons to make four trips a day to school, so instead of the old 7 period day we have changed to a 6 period day. School begins at 8:00 a.m. and ends at 12:30 p.m. with a recess of ten minutes every two forty minute periods. At two o'clock school reopens for those students who can come back. There is a general study hall until 3:30. The laboratory classes also meet at this time.

Another innovation is a ceremony every Friday at 12:35 in which Bachillerato students recite patriotic poems, the Cuban flag is saluted and the National Hymn is sung.

A new system has been devised for conduct marks. We have had so many requests from Defense Organizations for character reports of ex-students whose personality traits were not well remembered, that a new system seemed imperative. Mr. Davis and Dr. Gundlach devised the plan now being followed.

Each student is graded by each of his teachers on the following 8 traits: Industry, Leadership, Initiative, Cooperation, Judgement, Integrity, Emotional control and Personal appearance. His monthly conduct is figured from these. At the end of the year each student's score will be averaged for each trait and the result put on a graph which will be filed along with his permanent record card and a 35mm snapshot of the student taken when he leaves the school.

Every Friday night an informal party is given for the entertainment of the boarders. Day students come. Records are supplied and a live dance interspersed with games and refreshment ensues. These have been very successful and thoroughly enjoyed by all. (Why not let's have a few more of you "old grads" drop in some Friday nights? A few already have, and seemed to enjoy the informal festivities greatly.)

The Armed Services claimed several of our American teachers. Mr. and Mrs. MacGowan left in June 1942, and I believe Mr. MacGowan is in training for a

Petty Officer's rating in the Navy. Mr. Campbell also left at the same time and is now in training in Colorado for work with bombsights. Martha Henriquez, after a fling with friends in Washington, D.C. (She found a bed at an Aunt's house.) is now living in New York. She works for the C.B.S. in its Latin-American and Overseas Division.

Mr. Copithorne bid farewell to Beowulf for the duration in August 1942 and is now a private at the New England reception center of Fort Devens in Vt. and expects to be shipped soon to another training camp. His chief impression of Camp Devens is that it is considerably better behaved than an English IV class.

Mr. Cunningham, tearfully bid goodbye to Cuba in August, sadly mounted a Pan American Liner in charge of "a horrible, chattering tourist lady" and after a few weeks of freezing in Boston entered the service at Fort Devens. The camp is so big that, at last report he and Bill Copithorne had not even caught sight of each other. He hopes to be sent to Cubita Bella. His chief interest in army life seems to have been the kitchen. He says they start making breakfast toast at 10 p.m. on the night before and cook 1100 lbs of bacon per breakfast. It has also been reported that Mr. Powers (who recently married Frances Sutton) is doing defense work at M.I.T. Mr. Meston appeared in Havana for a short visit and Mr. Leinbach caught rheumatic fever in Mexico and we understand has part of one hand paralyzed.

The school administration so ably conducted by Mr. Cunningham last year is this season in the hands of Dr. Gundlach (now father of a second baby named Tom) and is progressing smoothly (both the administration and the baby). Dr. Polany has taken over most of the High School math. Mr. Davis, a friend of Mr. Baker has taken over the High School English and is doing a swell job. By the way, we no longer have our tennis courts: all athletics, under the direction of Mr. Riveiro take place at Parque José Martí.

Martha Fontanills is now Miss García's assistant taking the place of Sarah María García Tuñón who left shortly before her marriage.

We think we have a good bunch of students and congenial faculty this year and we are looking forward to a swell season.

Come around and see us sometime. Mr. Ruston's office is now in the room just in back of his old office.

TED VIAUX

Traditional Christmas Get-Together

On the night of Tuesday, December 29th, the main buildings of the school will be open from 9 to 12, for all Alumni and their guests. There will be dancing and if the war permits, food. In his efforts to increase the membership of the Association, Treasurer Max de Marchena is organizing a Membership Committee. All of you who are interested and willing to work see him at the party.

Inge Heilbronner
Class of 1944
The Ruston Yearbook 1944

IMPRESSIONS OF A FOREIGN STUDENT AT RUSTON

There is a proverb saying that all beginning is difficult, and another one "where there is a will, there is a way." The first one I have experienced frequently, but the second one my teachers taught me.

Well, believe me, I was pretty scared and confused the first time I came to Ruston. Everything was so strange, unusual, completely different from our European schools. And oh! I didn't understand what people were saying! What, for heaven's sake, did they mean? And when they kindly asked: "Tú no hablas español?" I tried to answer: "No just a little English" and thought: I still could understand much better if you would only talk with your hands! Mr. de la Cruz made my schedule. Schedule? I asked him, What is that? What was he going to do? And he wrote, 1st Period Shorthand, 2nd Period Bookkeeping, 3rd Business Arithmetic, and so on . . . I was beginning my commercial course.

But I was learning something more than only getting knowledge out of books and lessons. For the first time in my life I experienced comradeship, friendship. Yes, I may even say philanthropy, something new to us, who came from torn Europe, and I was seeing and wondering that in the midst of a world full of hate and struggle there could be a place like this. Whenever I didn't understand something, immediately somebody was ready to explain it over and over again, in English, in Spanish, until I finally understood. No teacher was impatient or unkind, and whenever I asked a classmate a question I never got an unwilling answer.

There have been times when I said: "I can't. It's too difficult! I really will never learn Shorthand or Spanish!" And to all this Mr. de la Cruz answered: "You can, of course you can. Why not, if you only want to?" And I wanted to and I could. Mr. de la Cruz has given me what I mostly lacked: self-reliance.

And now I am already in my last year. Taking dictation in Shorthand, studying Law and Accounting. Forgotten is shyness and timidity between periods, and in recess I have fun with the others.

We, students of commerce, are like a big family. Mr. and Mrs. de la Cruz are not only our teachers and educators, but are also our friends. We come to them with all our troubles, knowing they will understand and help us solve our difficulties.

A DAY IN THE COMMERCIAL DEPARTMENT

"Clang" goes the bell at half past eight!
It's woe to him who enters late,
For if excuses he should whine
"First law in business be on time"
Snaps out the Prof, "and get to work
There's nothing irks me like a shirk".

Bookkeeping first which we have found,
Just makes our heads spin round and round,
For it demands more than our talents
To make darned "balances" to "balance".

And soon the Prof begins to jaw
About that thing called "Business Law"
Talks learnedly of "fraud and tort"
Our juries, courts, things of that sort.
To save my life I can't see through it
All I can say "I didn't do it".

Then comes recess, we gaily chat
To free our minds, of this and that.
New clothes, the dance and of the boys
Who give school girls such pains and joys,
And then, unless we have gone broke
We brace for work with a good old coke.

Then dear Señora, watch in hand,
Is calling out her stern command.
She's watching us with vision keen,
"Come get to work at your machine".
We race along always in fright
That we can't spell the words just right.

*How happily ends our busy day
And when our books are filed away
There comes that feeling of content,
Which always crowns a day well spent
　If we have done our level best
　Tomorrow will care for the rest.*

*Now just a word of honest praise
For those who spend such busy days
In training us with patient care,
For useful futures bright and fair,
　Their every thought to help along
　And make us men and women strong.*

*So here's to de la Cruz and wife
Who taught us much of business life
And when to you we say goodbye
We promise you that we will try
　To do as we were taught to do
　In other words "live up to you".*

Mario Iglesias
Assistant Director of the Lower School, 1945-1961

RECUERDOS DE UN MAESTRO DEL RUSTON

Fue en aquel momento en 1945, que empecé a trabajar de maestro en el prestigioso Ruston Academy. Situado en G y Quinta, sus apacibles edificios de arquitectura colonial, han quedado hasta el presente grabados en mi memoria.

Sin embargo, lo que dejó en mi su más profunda huella, de lo cual me di cuenta desde el principio, fue el cambio notable que en el enfoque de mi carrera de maestro se iba operando. Diríamos en inglés, "it was a turning point in my approach to teaching".

Mis primeros contactos con Mr. y Mrs. Baker, con el profesorado en general, así como con el resto del personal, me hicieron sentir en un ambiente acogedor y culturalmente diverso. Diversidad cultural e intelectual que se extendía al alumnado y a sus familias.

Trabajar en el Ruston era un privilegio y una responsabilidad. Era la oportunidad, pero también con el compromiso, de participar en una empresa de altos vuelos académicos e ideológicos. Prestigio mantenido gracias al intercambio de ideas con aquellos que contribuían a funcionar como mentores, tanto del alumnado como entre el profesorado.

Hay que tener en cuenta que la calidad y dedicación de los alumnos eran inmejorables. Y, dedicarse a la enseñanza de alumnos altamente motivados, no solamente es un privilegio, sino una experiencia extraordinariamente estimulante, sobre todo para los maestros que aman su profesión.

Se contaba además con la cooperación de la familia de los alumnos. Aquellos que escogían el Ruston como escuela para sus hijos, propiciaban no solamente la adquisición de conocimientos, sino la asimilación de los valores cívicos y morales que deben existir en una institución dedicada a la educación de las generaciones futuras.

Jay Mallin
Class of 1945

RUSTON REMEMBRANCES

Raoul Goldhammer, a refugee from Romania, and Klaus Becker, a refugee from Germany, decided to publish a school newspaper for Ruston. It was 1943, the World War was in full sway, and a considerable number of refugees had found haven in Cuba.

Raoul and Klaus were friends of mine, and they asked me if I would be the treasurer for the enterprise and I agreed. Soon I found myself fully involved in preparing and publishing The Rustonian. The monthly was reproduced by mimeograph (remember them?). The two Europeans left Cuba for the United States, and in the following school term I was the sole editor.

Thus, at Ruston, began my journalism career, which would eventually span 50 years, six continents, 40 countries and some nine armed conflicts and various other aberrations of man and nature . . . .

Other memories of twelve years at Ruston:

Dr. Carlos Alvarado and his inseparable watch. He was the school's timekeeper, sending favored students to strike the chimes which signal a change of periods . . . .

Mr. Ruston ordering excavation of a rectangle on the raised portion of the patio to provide a realistic grave for the cemetery scene in Henry Eighth . . . .

Las chaperonas sitting around the patio during school dances . . . .

The school was a hodgepodge of adjoining buildings put together as the school expanded . . . .

Mr. Ruston sitting on a rocker in the foyer and minutely going over each student's monthly report card with him or her . . . .

The snack stand at one end of a long porch. It was managed by Abuelita . . . .

The Websters, including Medorah and Royal, arriving daily in the family fotingo . . . .

Margarita Gomez was a student during her father's presidency. One day she took her class on a tour of the Palacio Presidencial . . . .

Rubén "Papo" Batista and Zoe "Suzy" Prío were high school classmates when Rubén's father overthrew Zoe's uncle, who was President. Rubén made sure Zoe was unharmed . . . .

Dr. Bernard Gundlach throwing chalk to emphasize a point . . . .

After a few years at Ruston, the Americans spoke perfect Spanish, the Cubans perfect English....

Dr. Estela Agramonte making her students read Spanish classics, including two pages of Don Quijote in the original, medieval Spanish.

And the alumni went on to do great things: A number served with the American forces during World War II.... Robert Rediker, a brilliant student at Ruston and later at MIT, was a major participant in the development of the modern laser.... Modesto Maidique became president of Florida International University.... Bill Butler and his wife spent sixty-six days adrift on a raft in the Pacific when their sailboat was attacked and sunk by whales.... Beatriz Varela, professor at the University of New Orleans, became the foremost authority of Cuban words introduced into the Spanish language.

Gerry Smith
Class of 1945

PROFESORES QUE NOS INSPIRARON

Para mi el claustro del Ruston contenía dos superstars: la Agramonte y Agüero, ambos portando ilustres apellidos camagüeyanos.

Agüero nos enseñó Matemáticas a todos, desde Ingreso en adelante. Nunca sus clases fueron aburridas. Sabía combinar la enseñanza con sus cuentos, que nosotros le creíamos a pesar de que algunos deben haber sido exageraciones o puro invento. Tuvimos mucha suerte en tener ese guía durante los años en que nos estábamos formando. A mí me enseñó a pensar. No hay nada tan bello como una ecuación de segundo grado!

La Agramonte fue una enseñante incomparable. Nos burlábamos de ella por la forma en que pronunciaba La Chanson du Roland, pero era una maestra formidable que nos enseñó gramática y nos enseñó a escribir y a apreciar las joyas de la literatura castellana. Moça tan fermosa non vi en la frontera . . . Todavía a menudo me siento que me está mirando por encima del hombro cuando escribo y que me va a regañar si no pongo los acentos que tan mal me caen.

En tercer lugar (porque fue solo un curso) yo pongo a Mr Baker, que me enseñó English IV. Me faltaba ese credit y mi graduación había sido condicional. Ese verano del 45 me dedicó dos horas cada mañana para enseñarme Macbeth y las otras inglesadas. Tarea diaria: character sketch de Lady M, de mi abuela, de la derrota de Churchil por Atlee, etc. Revisados y comentados todos mis escritos diariamente. Otros en mis condiciones tuvieron a Mr Cunningham y otros, buenas gentes, pero no a la altura de Mr B.

En cuarto lugar para mi está Mrs Kitty Mitchell Hill, en English III. Era un personaje pintoresco con su programa en español en la TV, Mi Jardín, que mi madre veía encantada al mediodía, y su amor por The Flowering of New England, y su delirio con Longfellow y Evangeline, que yo no siempre compartía. Pero nos enseñó a apreciar el iambic pentameter, o como se llame, del Julius Caesar. Página y media del discurso de Mark Anthony, del que todavía recuerdo un buen trozo, y muchas otras "quotes" de las que he olvidado la mayoría. Siempre se me ha quedado el sabor a Shakespeare que Mrs H y Mr B me ofrecieron.

Esas eran las estrellas, pero los otros maestros también eran superiores. El Gallego Vázquez Gallo, que hizo el papel de Tartufo en el Teatro Universitario, republicano español y aspirante a artista, que nos enseñó Psicología y Economía Política. Juan Pujol Bibiloni, natural de Batabanó, con cuatro doctorados, quien nos decía que "Arbol que nace torcido, crece torcido", y luego me lo encontré de compañero mío en Primer Año de Derecho buscando un doctorado mas. Macuto

Neutrón Rexach, con quien nunca simpaticé pero que era buen maestro. Eduardo March, profesor de Geografía e Historia, ateo consumado, quien le iba a poner temporalmente a sus hijos—cuando los tuviera—Primero y Segundo, dejándolos que escogieran nombres definitivos después. En la Historia de Primer Año se estudiaban los Egipcios, los xxx, los Hebreos, los Griegos, etc. Cuando llegamos a los Hebreos, nos dijo que Jesús había sido un hombre como otro cualquiera y me hizo polvo la creencia religiosa que yo tenía a los 14 años. Creencia que es como la virginidad: una vez que se pierde no se recupera. March tuvo una gran influencia sobre mi, pero era un enseñante de primera a quien yo admiraba y respetaba.

Con mi memoria podrida como la tengo estoy seguro que se me olvida alguien. Sé que se me ha olvidado el nombre de la civilización que se desarrolló en el Líbano, los que inventaron el dinero y comerciaron por todo el Mediterráneo. En cuanto haya tocado el SEND lo recordaré. [Efectivamente, los Fenicios]

Párrafo aparte hay que dedicarle al inspirador de todos esos buenos maestros, a Mr Hiram H Ruston. Ya en mi época él no enseñaba en un aula, pero se sentaba en aquel gran salón lleno de sillones para revisar las notas mensuales de todos los alumnos y ponerle asteríscos al lado de las notas altas. Yo no conozco ninguna escuela o centro de enseñanza donde el Director trate con todos y cada uno de los alumnos mensualmente. Mr Ruston era único.

Y el Profesor Alvarado, con quien todos tuvimos que tratar. Le enseñaba español a los americanos. A mi me tuvo mis primeros dos meses en una de sus clases porque yo me llamaba Jerry Smith. Como yo era muy tímido no protestaba, pensando que esa era la regla de mi nuevo colegio, pero no me interesaban los subjuntivos de los que él hablaba.

Que nostalgia me produce el hablar de todas esas cosas!

Beatriz Varela
Class of 1945

I shall never stop thanking my dear parents for having sent me to such a wonderful school as Ruston Academy. As a scholar and as an academician, I have studied at the University of Havana, at the Catholic University of Santo Tomas de Villanueva, at Tulane University in New Orleans, at the Universidad Complutense of Madrid, at the Oficina Internacional de Información y Observación del Español (OFINES) in Madrid. However, even though I take great pride in what I learned while attending these universities, my true formation comes from my Ruston years: first grade through high school and fourth year of "Bachillerato" (Ruston did not have then a fifth year of "Bachillerato", so nearly all graduates of Ruston attended the Instituto del Vedado to fulfill the last college requirement before reaching the university level.)

As an elementary and intermediate student, I remember, sometimes with affection, other times with a little fear, several of my Ruston teachers. Mrs. Prieto, first grade, was famous for being extremely strict and for insisting that everyone learn. After one class with Mrs. Prieto, I came home saying hello to my family in English, a language that I was just beginning to learn. Mrs. Bryon, my second grade teacher, was just as rigorous and as good an instructor as Mrs. Prieto. Teaching Spanish was Mr. Alvarado, whose two daughters were classmates of mine. The students used to make fun of him because he ranked their seats by grades, so there was a constant place changing in his class. He ended the period by calling the roll followed by the grades. For example, he would state: "Joe Doc, excelente, conducta excelente", or "Mary Smith, notable, conducta suspenso".

At the intermediate level, we had reached the stage where we no longer feared our teachers but wanted to learn more from them and become closer to their teachings. All Rustonians remember with great affection Mrs. Hill, Mrs. McMasters, and Madame Menassé, who also taught high school. Every time I listen to the music of Gilbert and Sullivan, the image of Mrs. Hill, comes to my mind, with her red hair, while trying to teach us how to follow the rhythm of the melody with the words of the operetta. Additionally, Mrs. Hill also directed an unusual play The Pinafore by Gilbert and Sullivan. Mrs. Mc's green eyes lightened whenever she explained Evangeline, Hiawatha, or Rip Van Winkle, and her lectures enriched all of us. And last but not least was our superb French teacher, Madame Menasse. The very first day of class she warned the students that French was the only language allowed in the classroom. When you did not know how to say something in French, you had to raise your hand. Once Madame had translated the question, everyone had to learn it. Any student using English or Spanish had to pay a fine, which was used to buy books in French. The four years of French that I took at Ruston with Madame Menassé enabled me to pass successfully the French reading exam required in graduate school at Tulane University. Let me add that I am not the only one praising Madame Menassé. Even those students lacking a gift for language learning, acquired fluency in the French language classes of Madame.

Mr. Ruston, the founder of the school, used to sit in a rocking chair in the large living room of the school situated at G and 5th St., to check the monthly report cards of each student. Each class was ushered into the parlor and each one exchanged rocking chairs until he or she arrived at the one beside Mr. Ruston who, pen in hand, checked the grades of every report card. He praised the good grades and encouraged each student to improve the not so good ones. Mr. Ruston was also well known as a director of plays. His death was a terrible loss for educators, parents, students and the entire city of Havana. Fortunately, his sister Martha, was able to find the best successor in James D. Baker, of whom I shall speak again.

At the "Bachillerato" and high school levels, there are many instructors who deserve to be recognized. Bernard Gundlach and Maria Quintero taught mathematics and Latin, respectively, at the high school levels. Teaching English at the same level were Copithorne, Cunningham and Baker. The thorough analyses of Shakespearean plays, especially As You Like It, Hamlet, King Lear and Macbeth made by Mr. Baker in his classes, have remained fresh in my mind, as have the regular visits to his home to discuss the masterpieces of English literature. Mrs. Baker always welcomed all of us and spoiled us by offering the always hungry students delicious homemade cookies and refreshments. Mrs. Baker directed the school chorus, which always performed at Christmas and other school activities.

In "Bachillerato", as was usually the case in all departments at Ruston Academy, there were excellent teachers. Eduardo March taught geography, anatomy and biology, and later became a physician; Antonio Vásquez was in charge of history and Spanish grammar; Eduardo Rexach dealt with chemistry, geology, botany and zoology; Juan Pujol was responsible for civics. I have deliberately left for last, Estela Agramonte and Arístides Agüero, since they were very unique, colorful in their explanations and knowledgeable. Agramonte, who in later years became the head of the "Bachillerato" department, taught all the literature courses in high school and also in "Bachillerato". Her students loved and admired her, in spite of the fact that they enjoyed making fun of her allergy to chalk dust. Agüero was responsible for mathematics and physics. He used to send his students to the blackboard and if they could not solve the mathematical problem, he would cross his hands with open fingers in front of his face, and say "My cook Betsy would have solved that problem immediately. You, however, could have been locked in a cage with a gorilla, and a bunch of bananas high on the cage and a ladder. Well, the gorilla would reach the bananas with the ladder *long before you."* Even though the student at the blackboard was trembling, he or she understood Agüero's mocking and knew that the solution of the equation was going to be explained soon. Before starting all of his classes, Aguero would narrate some fanciful and imaginary adventures: being a "descendant of Jupiter", he swam underwater every morning from the Bay of Havana to the Morro Castle. Let me finish by saying that Arístides Agüero really prepared his classes well, and therefore he was always congratulated by the Instituto del Vedado when the grades of his "Bachillerato" students came.

The extra-curricular activities at Ruston Academy were numerous. There was an annual field day with all sorts of games and competitions. We played basketball, flag-football, softball, track, volleyball and enjoyed competing against other school teams.

After I received my doctorate from the University of Havana and also from the Catholic University of Santo Tomás de Villanueva, Dr. Estela Agramonte hired me to teach Spanish grammar and literature to Ruston "Bachillerato" students. I had been away from my dear school for nearly ten years, and I was thrilled to return, this time, as an instructor. My classes were always well prepared, even though the alert and witty students, who realized that I was new at my job, would ask me tough questions from a chapter not due for that day. However, I not only survived but became an excellent teacher, thanks to their inquisitive minds. Nothing pleases me more than to attend the Ruston reunions in Miami, where I have the pleasure of meeting my former classmates and students and also my colleagues, with whom I have established close friendships. Practically all Ruston students have successfully completed different careers at elite universities like MIT, Harvard, Yale, Columbia, University of Virginia, University of California at Davis, Vassar, Tulane.

Thanks to the efforts of the Baker family, Ruston now had a beautiful new school in the residential area called Biltmore in Havana. It was designed to house all departments: elementary with large kindergarten and pre-primary classrooms; intermediate, high school and "Bachillerato". It saddened me when my family and I had to leave Cuba because of the Communist regime of Fidel Castro. I regretted that my son George, who was only able to complete kindergarten and pre-primary, would never be able to benefit from a Ruston education.

With pleasure and great pride I repeat that my main education came from Ruston Academy, a bi-lingual school. Whatever I have accomplished in my life as a professor, as an author (four books and thirty articles), as a life member of the Academia Norteamericana de la Lengua Española (elected 1993), and as a Corresponding Academician of the Real Academia Española (1994, after I presented my acceptance speech at Columbia University to become an Académica de Número), I attribute to the formation and knowledge acquired at Ruston Academy: small classes, interesting cultural exchanges between students and teachers, love of learning and freedom to learn. Ruston was and is a family to all of us. My hope is that the school will be able to reopen when Cuba is free again.

Robert Allen
Class of 1946

RUSTON IN THE MID-1940s

The mid-1940's was an interesting time, hard for anyone to imagine who did not live through them. It was a time of war, of victory and of building hopes and institutions for peace. For a U.S. national male teenager, it was a time for great patriotism, for great fear, and, in the end, of optimism for the future. All of these affected me as I lived in Havana from mid-1944 to mid-1946, first with parents and later as an 'interno' at the school.

Ruston, too, was a school reflecting the times. About a third of the students were US citizens, some the traditional sons and daughters of long term resident businessmen and other expatriates, some the very transient dependents of military personnel on the island, and me, long-term expatriate, caught on the island, unable to rejoin my family until the war ended. Another third of the student body were the children of Cuban families with strong US ties that sought a US based education for their children. And, finally, about a third of the students were from families of refugees from Hitler's atrocities, denied refuge in the United States, yet hoping they and/or their children would eventually find a home in the United States and seeking an education for their children that would help assure it. To a somewhat lesser degree, the faculty and staff reflected the same groupings.

This mixture coexisted in Ruston with remarkable harmony, a tribute to the school. There was little squabbling with strong friendships developing across the different groups. How this came about, I believe, was a result of the school being a place where most liked to be, not a place we felt we had to be. Students and faculty could be found puttering around the place long after school hours—frequently working on projects not directly related to studies—well do I remember the monstrous Tesla coil Dr. Gundlach and students built, the hours spent in the darkroom, and working on plays (not just the acting and the producing, but fabricating the equipment needed).

Ruston was not a place of luxury. When my local board decides to up my school taxes again, for such items as a $60,000 mat for the wrestling team, or a multi-million dollar renovation of the perfectly adequate high school, I think of us in a series of somewhat dilapidated, modest Cuban homes, interspersed with residences over several city blocks, with classes wherever desks and chairs could be stuffed. Mats for a wrestling team? What wrestling team? What gym? . . . more like long trolley rides to the "Mothers' Club" for baseball, swimming in a "cut-out" in the coral rock (dangerous, but fun.). Multi-million dollar cafeteria facility? Never, but we all got fed through a series of rapid conversions of patios into dining rooms. It was not a place of luxury, but a place of warmth, stimulation, and participation.

Did we receive an inadequate education? Were we somehow deprived? Just look at what the students of that time did after they graduated.

Kitty Hill
English teacher, 1936-1949
The Columns 1948

A LETTER FROM GRETCHEN

    A letter from Gretchen came today with the comforting news that she has at last found home in the Promised Land at which all refugees gaze longingly. "'The feeling not to move in the next future", she writes, "is really a very fine feeling". That poignant phrase recalls the story of her family. Miraculously young Gretchen survived, her tender blonde beauty blossoming with faith in the circle of returning springtides.

    With a lump in my throat I open my desk to put away Gretchen's letter in a file marked "Teacher's Tonic". Within are the letters and pictures and compositions which have given me a lift on discouraging days. Most of my "tonic" has a foreign label.

    Here is a composition, written with fastidious exactness, about "The Ancient Dragon Festival", and it is signed merely "Tsi". Today his bright almond eyes are gazing raptly up at some lucky teacher in far-away Turkey. Tsi was perhaps too good.

    In this picture Josef was clad for his Bar Mitzvah in silk topper, Eton jacket, and white kid gloves. Evidently he had tried to assume the solemnity proper to the ceremony, but the impish twinkle of his irrepressible high spirits is unquenchable. As his English vocabulary grew, he regaled us with tales of his last months in Rumania . . . . and how a brave teacher had conducted his last classes in a tiny dark bathroom.

    "En cet heureux Dimanche, 22 Fevrier" is the heading of a graceful little French poem for my birthday, a poem written by a hand which will some day write famous books . . . . I am sure of it. François escaped from Paris when he was too young to realize just what was happening, but the terrified little boy whispered, "Maman, something is jumping inside me!" And his young mother replied, "That is the loyal heart of a true little Frenchman!" A true Frenchman he has remained, expressing his nostalgia in charming little word-pictures of this motherland.

    How vividly I recall the day when Igor and his brother came out to the farm to make all these photographs for me! How cleverly they drew the pictures and decorated the pages with amusing little sketches, such as this one of a savage popping his startled head out of the big earthen jar in the garden.

"*Escape with a Parambulator*" is the title of Maryla's composition, with its stark realism of road-side scenes, when the precious baby carriage was hastily concealed in the underbrush while the fleeing family made for freedom. No wonder Maryla clasped to her breast the old rag doll, for under the doll's hair were hidden the few jewels which would purchase their way to freedom from Poland's conquerors.

This picture of a fairy-tale castle, surrounded by terraced gardens and well-groomed parks, is the ancient "schloss" where Elizabetka's family lived for generations, until one day they could no longer remain within those ivy clad towers. I remember how Elizabetka looked on that first day in my Basic English class . . . round, baby face, surrounded by black corkscrew curls, and an air of utter bewilderment, for although she spoke Yugoslav, Russian and German, she knew not one word of English or Spanish. Her handsome brother, Vladimir, served as a bridge of understanding between us, for he could speak French. Patiently we built up her vocabulary, through French and Yugoslav into Basic English, and within a few months we were chatting together quite freely. One Sunday afternoon they brought their mother out to the farm, and I sent Elizabetka out to gather flowers. Later I found her in the garden, her eyes bright with tears, as she buried her flushed face in the sweet peas. "Oh, I can smell the springtime now at the castle! I wonder who is there to breathe the perfume of the lilacs? Every year, when the first violets bloomed, we threw open our park so every one could enjoy the spring flowers!" And then she opened her purse and gave me this picture of their castle.

Most precious of my souvenirs is a ribbon rosette clasp with the double-eagle crest of Yugoslavia. It will always remind me of Niinotschka's big eyes as she told me, "One so good English bishop came to Belgrade, but the secret police took pictures of all the people who went to see him in the church. My little schoolmate was identified and chained in a cell of water, because she had defied them. When we could no longer live under Tito's rule, one so brave American aviator save our life and we keep traveling till we reach Cuba. But next month our permission to remain here is finish, and if the quota number does not come to let us enter America, my mother and her three daughters will have to find some way to live suspended in the air . . . for no country will take us!"

As I close the file of "Teacher's Tonic", I wonder if I have been the teacher after all. It seems to me that I have learned from these pupils far more than I could ever teach them. They scarcely need teachers at all, for they eagerly reach out to absorb all the knowledge they can soak up. By plunging simultaneously into both English and Spanish they have found that one can learn to speak a language quickly, before bothering with rules and written exercises. They have spoiled me forever by their sympathetic response to literature, and by the keen observation and lively imagination which animates their composition.

Among the American Joes and Marys, the Cuban Josés and Marías, the European Josefs and Marylas are inextricably interwoven—and none of them are "foreigners" in Ruston Academy. They have inspired us all with their examples of uncomplaining fortitude, of gracious adaptability, and of ardent appreciation. As our little group of refugee students becomes smaller, we eagerly await the letters which mark the end of their years of wandering, rejoicing in such poignant messages as Gretchen's: "The feeling not to move again in the next future is really a very fine feeling."

Annie Ludlum
Class of 1949

One afternoon sitting in study hall outside Dr. Gundlach's classroom, I had a moment of euphoric clarity: I realized that I would never be happier than I was right then.

I was reading Anna Karenina and I had chapters and chapters still in store. Later in the day I was to rehearse my role of Ariel in The Tempest. And I had with me a letter from the most dazzling Cuban youth who ever danced the bote.

I was correct. I have been as happy since, but never any happier.

What are the Ruston elements in that moment? The old Vedado building which fostered awareness of and affection for our entire community, as well as appreciation of the city beyond the school; faculty encouragement of intellectual challenge; institutional commitment to artistic endeavors; recognition of the validity of each individual's feelings.

As I attended Ruston for only my first two years of high school (1945-7), I can't distinguish between those aspects of my later life which were inspired solely by my Ruston stay and those for which the seeds had already been planted and for which Ruston provided a nurturing environment. But I've ended up being an actress and a playwright (and occasional teacher and librarian). My published plays deal with the struggles of people who are considered moral as they try to do what they themselves believe to be the right thing. Spanish is the first language of many of my characters.

So—long-term Ruston influence? Come on—it permeates work. Now, if I could just live in a house with a patio and the sound of bongos and scent of . . .

Ah, well, Jim Baker, I am eternally grateful for my Ruston days and consider all of us lucky who passed through the columns and became, however briefly, part of Ruston Academy.

Unidentified Member of the Class of 1951

 I remember Hal Neuendorf's unique way of keeping track of how you were doing in his class. He used a = and—system in a little black book and circled particularly outstanding contributions or gaffes. He always left the book open and we were forever peeking to see if we were participating enough and had enough pluses to offset the inevitable minus. His method of teaching English, having each of us take turns leading a class discussion on either a poem or a short story, was novel and incredibly effective. We learned to dig deep for all the meaning in the work because we knew he gave heavy emphasis to these efforts in our final grades. Interestingly, at the same time we got a tremendous lesson in public speaking and leading a group discussion. He was simply the best English Literature teacher I ever had. That includes my years in college. He was a heck of a history teacher also!!!!

 I also recall the Shakespearean play, I believe it was the comedy Much Ado About Nothing on the patio outside of Mr. Baker's office in my Junior year. It was the first Shakespearean play I had ever seen, and it had a huge impact on me. I remember it being quite good.

The Havana Post
Supplement
February 8, 1953

Ruston's Cultural Program

Many phases of the school activities such as reading of English, Spanish and French literature; reading writing and producing plays; work with puppets; classes in chorus and music appreciation are organized to help develop the child's imagination and to give him a broad cultural background and a capacity to enjoy music and the arts.

Emphasis on the Development of Responsible Citizens for a Democracy

Since the major function of a school in a democracy is to produce adults prepared for their responsibilities as citizens, the Academy believes that the experiences of the past two decades outline some of her principal functions. Recent events emphasize the role that education plays in influencing the thinking of people and helps us to appreciate that democracy is a matter of habits of thinking and methods of solving problems. The breakdown of democratic processes that led to the catastrophe of World War II shows that if democracy is to survive, it must exist first in the evaluation processes of the mature, responsible adults who compose society.

Therefore, education at the primary and secondary level should be a process of stimulating and guiding the development of minds that are trained, disciplined tools, capable of doing independent work. In attempting to achieve this goal, teachers place emphasis upon the understanding evaluation of materials studied, upon the application of principles learned so that the students may not confuse encyclopedic information with understanding. The Academy believes that it is necessary to give children experience in thinking for themselves, in making a critical analysis of material from various sources if we are to provide men and women with the judgment necessary to solve present-day economic, political and international problems where even the best solution is a compromise and an adjustment of many conflicting points of view and interests. Once she has helped students determine basic values; her problem is to teach them how to tackle and solve problems, how to think straight more than what to think.

In order that an individual may grow from a self-centered child to a mature adult, it is necessary that he understand the bonds of mutual interest and cooperation that unite him with all mankind. Much attention, therefore, is given to helping develop an understanding of their obligations to others, awakening in them a sense of duty to others and to their community and country.

Realizing that a productive adult must possess initiative and responsibility, the school begins to develop those traits in the first grade. Numerous opportunities are provided within the classroom and in extra-curricular activities for children to organize and carry out projects on their own. Teachers work constantly to develop the individual's habits and capacities for executing and completing as well as for dreaming and planning.

Because the greatest need of our day is for capable, well-trained, public-spirited leaders, every available opportunity in the classroom, in extra-curricular activities and on the sport fields is used to develop children's potential leadership and to create in them the realization that a good leader must think first of all his team, his group, rather than of himself.

Results

A study of the reports of Ruston graduates in American colleges showed that their academic achievement in the freshman year equaled or excelled their records at Ruston.

In Cuba secondary education the work of the Ruston Bachillerato Deparment merited official recognition and praise from the examining boards of the Instituto del Vedado.

Ruston Contribution to Cuba

A. Cuban students at Ruston have the opportunity to learn from North American teachers and to study under American methods of education without the double risks involved in sending them to the North for extended study. Those risks are: first, that they will not develop thorough mastery of their native tongue; second, that the student who lives long abroad will lose contact with his home and family and miss something of the deep love for his homeland that is the birthright of every child.
B. Ruston cooperates in making available in Cuba much of the wealth of instruction materials and pedagogical procedures that is being produced as a result of the experiments and research of hundred of colleges and universities in the North.
C. Scholarships are granted to 8 per cent of the students.

D. Although founded and directed by Americans, the school in a true sense exists for the benefit of Cuba and Cubans.

1. 65% of her students are Cubans.
2. 72% of her teachers are Cubans.
3. As the school is now a non-profit foundation, the prosperity of the school will be a direct benefit to Cuba
4. The school has always emphasized the value of Cuban culture and attempted to awaken Cuban students to the challenge presented by the great potentialities of their rich land. It has been Ruston's desire to develop in students the most valuable type of patriotism, that which causes one to dedicate his life to working for his country to help develop her resources
5. The results of the Academy's efforts to produce leaders in all fields of national life is reflected in the work of her graduates who are distinguishing themselves in professions and in the business world.

Ruston—An Educational United Nations

A. The Ruston student body is always very cosmopolitan with representatives of from ten to twenty different nations. Her students range from the children of presidents, royal families, and diplomats to penniless victims of war.
B. One of the most encouraging evidences of the beneficial results of this meeting of nationalities and cultures is the absence of the prejudices that too often separate people. It warms one's heart to see youngsters going out of their way to welcome a shy Chinese girl and teach her to play volleyball with a mixed group of boys and girls, or to watch the way ten-year olds can use smiles and sign language to help a Scandinavian boy who can speak neither English nor Spanish.

Religious tolerance is similarly shown as Jews join Christians in Christmas celebrations, and Protestants attend the confirmation ceremonies of their Catholic friends.

Even more satisfying is the extent to which students leave behind their political differences when they enter the school.

Last year during the political crisis the fact that members of the families of the three outstanding political leaders were studying in the same department at Ruston presented no problem for the students involved or for their friends.

The democratic spirit of the school is reflected in the absence of lines of social or financial position. No distinctions exist between the wealthiest girl or boy in *school and a scholarship student. Often the latter are outstanding leaders in activities and among the most popular students in their groups. This democratic spirit is reflected by the following incidents. Last year when one of the servants of the school was dying in the hospital, his little daughter was staying with one of her classmates, the niece of the President. At the same time Rubén Batista and the son of the school gardener were working together on a committee of the Student Council. It would be difficult to say which was more popular with the class he represented.*

Joan Beaulac
Class of 1955

Both Noel and I were in Mrs. Baker's madrigal group that met at lunch time and our rehearsal hours were pleasant interludes in my miserable schooldays. She was exceptionally kind and spent a lot of time and energy on her singers—the general chorus, too, of course, but how I relished our lunchtime madrigal practices.

Dear Boris Goldenberg introduced us to foreign film (in the early '50s) and showed films during one lunch hour a week—a lunch hour not committed to singing practice. The films were well chosen lessons that the world is more than our individual personal realities. Wonderful Boris (who could consume an entire bottle of coke in one swallow!) agreed to give me a passing grade in 2nd year french on condition that I never embarrass him by signing up for french again (we were moving to Chile—did he have a reputation there?). No wonder I worshipped him! I've kept my word to him for the past 45 years. And, naturally, I love trying out my fractured french when I travel!! Mais biensur! Six months don't go by without my remembering him with a smile.

Hal Neuendorf listened when students talked. He recommended books to me that were comforting, stimulating, mind-expanding. The time I spent with the books he chose for me was healing.

I delighted in my occasional skip-outs to the Malecon. The rocks on the other side of the wall came almost up to street level and it was easy to clamber down to where bits of sealife would be caught in the craggy hollows. I wonder if Mr. Baker remembers when I brought back a few crabs and let them loose in his office when he'd stepped out. Perhaps the crabs scurried through the bars out to the "study hall/lunch room" area before he returned.

I liked the mellow old building where "high school" held most of its classes. What was that building's role in the world before it was a school? Although I grew up in Latin America I never took courtyards for granted. And I still think they're nifty. I'll never forget a dance at Ruston where las madrecitas, las tias, las abuelitas sat lined up against the wall of the front courtyard, quietly watching "que los tin-eichers se portaran todos bien". And what a nice little stage that was. Of course, the smaller courtyard with its coke machine was the best place for really important conversations.

Like zillions of youngsters of that age, I profoundly hated school, hated home, hated being ordered about by people, who, by some accident, had been born twenty years before me. But since I first stumbled upon the "Ruston site" I've been recalling many wonderful things that happened to me during my two short years of adolescent rage and desperation in Havana.

Denny Baker
Class of 1956

In thinking back on the learning experience at the school there are several characteristics that go as far back as I can remember. The two most prominent are a healthy challenge for each to do his personal best and a striving for disciplined thinking. In the high school years these stimuli became a more prominent part of our classes. The emphases on efficient reading and clear writing sharpened these important skills. In addition, many of the high school classes clearly provided advanced levels of content, as I discovered once I reached college.

There are many examples of the high goals of classes. Included in these are Marta Ferrer's math, Hal Neuendorf and Jim Baker's English classes, Hilda Perera's Spanish literature and Boris Goldenberg's history. It is hard to define specifically what made each of these teachers excel but each certainly had the right stuff.

In a nonacademic area, the school not only emphasized bi-lingual skills but also had the unstated mission of promoting bi-culturalism. Equal emphasis was given to Cuban and American history, traditions and cultural foibles.

It was not until I returned to the United States as a college freshman that I appreciated the great advantage I had in many situations of always looking at issues from more than one point of view. Fortunately, this is a perspective I have retained through my life.

The full benefit of my academic preparation became obvious in college and medical school and contributed to achievements in later years. The work discipline developed by many of my Ruston classes was critical in coping with the heavy demands I encountered. A particular benefit was my experience in developing my thoughts into a coherent paper.

Judy Benson
Class of 1956

This is more of a recollection of an amazing assignment that has stayed with me all these years. Back when I was in the ninth grade, which means about 1952, I brought home an English assignment that even got my parents involved. The assignment was to read a biography by Emil Ludwig, and then write a paper on Emil Ludwig. What kind of man was he to have chosen his subject, and then what did he choose to emphasize, minimize, and so on. My parents got into the act by reading the book after I had, and we had many discussions, long after I had submitted the paper.

Ruston was a school not only for the students, but their families. And these were involved in ways beyond the norm. It was a truly special place at a special time. Thank you, Mr. Baker, for the lifetime education as well as the lifetime memories.

Agustín Ríos
Class of 1956

There are many good memories from Ruston. I find it amazing that some of my best friends now are schoolmates from over forty-five years ago. More importantly, I married one!

One of my fondest memories from Ruston is the help I got from teachers in 1955, when I decided to skip my senior year before going to the university. You may remember that Tony de Cardenas and I wanted to come to universities in the U.S. to study engineering without completing our senior year. We elected different paths. Tony studied the subjects for "quinto año de bachillerato" on his own and passed the institute exams. I elected to take the College Board achievement tests, and I needed a lot of help.

At that time, Dra. Marta Ferrer taught a math course that prepared students to take the math achievement test. You suggested that I sit in. It was a small group, and Dra. Ferrer would not only spend time with the group during school hours, but would meet the group in her house after hours and on Saturdays. Soon, I found that she would spend time teaching me, on weekends, in order to bring me up to the level of proficiency that she thought I should have to take the exam and she had high standards. I was not even a student in her class! As a result of her attention and effort, I was able to enter MIT as a freshman without having had my senior year. She was an absolutely dedicated and extraordinary teacher who had a profound influence on how life turned out for me.

After I was admitted to MIT, Dr. Aldo Forte, who was the physics teacher in bachillerato approached me and said that I would need to learn some calculus if I wanted to succeed in my first year at MIT. He used to teach the first-year calculus course at the University of Havana, and he volunteered to get together with me after hours at the university. We had several meetings, during which he directed me to study certain topics and answered questions I had on the subject.

At that time, I did not understand, as I do now, the significance of the attention I was getting from these teachers, during their free time, with no remuneration involved. These were truly exceptional teachers.

Harry Skilton
Class of 1956

You may recall that *Profesora Ferrer* in teaching her college level math course on Saturday in her home would insist that we sit at her dining room table and take a test of 60 questions in one hour. In order to make sure we concentrated she had her recently born infant crawl around and mess up our papers.

I will always be amazed at the fact that *Profesora Ferrer* would outline from scratch without a text book the major theorems that we were covering on that particular Saturday class. We were all required to have a binder, and she used to rotate our binders. I still have my binder somewhere in a box with her derivation of the theory of differential calculus.

Professor Neuendorf—He got a rowdy junior high school class to accept poetry in his English literature class by having us listen to tapes of folk singers.

Professor Goldenberg—He instilled in us a love for the classics and philosophy during his Socratic luncheon discussions, on the veranda of the new school building in the Alturas del Biltmore.

Mrs. Baker—How she would take a bunch of rowdy young men who could not read a single note and convince them to join the chorus and madrigal. I for one could never read notes, and she would spend time teaching me my part.

At the new school, on the first day of the newly instituted girls' gym period we were kept behind the gate. I'm amazed that we didn't have chaperones too.

The superior civil engineering feat of our sophomore male class was to actually dig a hole through the outside fence of the study hall, in the old Vedado building, in order to make it to the swimming pool of the hotel next door.

My first composition in your senior class of language and thought and action where I received a minus (!!) 275 for English and subsequently had to take a summer course in order to graduate.

Graciela Rodríguez
Class of 1956

I have quite a few memories! Here are some of them:

Mr. Neuendorf's junior English class: In order to make grammar tests a little less dry, he would write gossipy sentences, spicing them with juicy tid-bits of who was romantically involved with whom (see, I haven't forgotten how to use subjective and objective pronouns!).

Mr. Baker's senior English class: The famous (infamous?) Hayakawa's Language in Thought and Action. Few high school courses have helped me more in life. It taught me how to think; the relative and dangerous value of advertisement; how to distinguish truth from fabricated truth; how cow 1 was not cow 2; and so many more important lessons, such as listening to a master teacher conduct a class.

Mr. Goldenberg's lunch seminar: Mr. Goldenberg held a seminar on Kant during lunch in the terraza of the building right over the kitchen in the new school en Alturas del Country. He gave his lunch time in a busy schedule to sit with a few seniors and discuss Kantian philosophy.

Mr. Ruff's square dancing class: Another teacher who gave time during lunch was Mr. Ruff. He taught us square dancing, which for the Cuban students was a novelty. He not only taught the steps, but also taught us the history of this American dance form.

Dra. González-Recio: She taught her senior Latin American history class using literature. This was not commonly done in the 50's, and made the class very enjoyable. I recall she also did that for her Modern European class, and her students had to get written permission from their parents in order to read "mature" books.

Nina's sewing class: Nina, our bus 4 chaperona, taught a group of 4th grade girls (1948) how to make pillowcases and embroider them, and she also darned our nylons. What makes this remarkable to me is that she was very involved in our lives, teaching us manners and talking with us frequently; one could always go to her for advice and comfort.

Sylvia Upmann
Class of 1957

I loved acting. Since my Mom, Cuqui Ponce de León, was a director, I grew up in the artistic field. So I decided that "Public Speaking" with Mr. Neuendorf would be a cinch. Little did I figure how different it would be from acting and difficult it would be for me to stand in front of a group of people, look at their faces, and just say what I wanted to say with a purpose and in a way that would influence the group and keep them interested. And of course, Mr. Neuendorf would sit in the last row in the middle, with his head sticking about one foot above everyone elses heads and just staring at me. While giving my first speech, I was fidgeting with a rubber band around my fingers, and no they weren't hurting but they were turning purple and I was really nervous. So of course, Mr. Neuendorf puts this paper in front of his face that reads "You are losing your fingers, they are turning a beautiful purple blue". I looked at my fingers and realized how much energy I was wasting on them. I learned that in public speaking eye contact is extremely important, and that your hand and body language should follow what you are saying and not detract from your message. Up to this day, there is not one time when I have to give a seminar, or presentation, I don't see Mr. Neuendorf sitting in the last row with his head one foot taller than the rest.

Another anecdote comes from a writing composition class with Mr. Jim Baker. Perlita Menocal had just joined our class for the last year so as to graduate with us from Bachillerato. She had just come back from the United States, where she had graduated from High School. And here comes her first composition graded by Mr. Baker for a "-125 points". We were in awe! How could she get that grade when she had completed her High School studies in the USA? Another big lesson, Perlita used many direct translations from Spanish to English, and that was a "NO! NO!". So almost immediately all our minds started working laboriously so as not to get a "-125 points" in ours.

Ruston was a fun place. I used to go home for lunch and could not wait to get back to school because lunch time was when some of the fun activities took place. The same, believe it or not, was true of the school's Saturday detention program. Those who accumulated a certain number of demerits had to work them off on Saturday mornings at the new school. I felt deprived because my behavior normally was not such as to warrant the accumulation of the necessary points. It did not make sense that you should have to behave badly to get assigned the fun activities of washing windows and pulling weeds with your friends.

Ruston's biggest influence on my life was teaching me to communicate with people from other countries with respect, and paying attention to what they want to say. Communication, a yearning to keep on learning, and a willingness to accept other people's philosophies has meant a lot to me. I reach out to many different kinds of people, and it makes me feel really good. But then I had a good start!

Olga Karman
Class of 1958

I remember most clearly the skills Ruston teachers taught me. These teachers made a writer out of me both in English and Spanish. Memories of these excellent teachers influence my teaching today. I am as exacting as they were; and, like them, I balance high expectations with dedication to students' intellectual growth. I respect their minds in the way our teachers at Ruston respected ours. I think of teaching as "forming" or "molding" not as filling empty minds.

I remember the self-discipline and hard work. After Ruston, all work was comparatively easy. I never worked that hard again, except off-and-on at Harvard.

I remember Mr. Baker's Senior English class. He made us very sensitive to the uses and misuses of language. The latter became very prevalent after 1959. We graduates often communicated later that what we had learned in this class helped us to see through the manipulation of thoughts and words in the years that followed 1959. I remember the way my experiences at Ruston affected my personal goals. There was no doubt that we would go to college and excel! Be professionals and excel! That was what we had been taught to aim for and value!

Chris Baker
Class of 1959

EL PATIO DEL INTERMEDIATE

Going to grades 4 to 6 at Ruston without a patio would have been a tragedy. The patio was the center of activity at recess and at lunch and the place where many valuable lessons were learned. This was where many of us developed our yo-yo prowess until these were banned as dangerous flying objects due to broken strings resulting from our efforts to impress each other with our round-the-world skills. It was where many of us pursued our first loves. It was also where acto cívico activities and plays were held. Where many of us first worked on our basketball skills driving toward a basket that was unforgiving—it was mounted on one of the walls of the patio.

LAS BOMBITAS ATOMICAS

In Intermediate, volleyball in the patio was the center of our competitive beings at lunchtime. We lived for it—I know this to be a fact for the boys and suspect it to have been true for many of the girls as well. We boys were convinced that we were invincible and did not want to play with the girls. Not approving of this situation, Mario Iglesias organized what he called Las Bombitas Atómicas—a team of girls which he captained. He taught us in doing so that brute force did not always win over discipline and team work. The Bombitas did in fact beat the boys and we had to "eat crow" from time to time. I still remember some of the Bombita's stars—Isabel Quilez, Lourdes Valentiner, Vicky Samson, Betsy Garber, Symmie Landreth . . . . I bet they still could take us in a few games today.

THE NEXT DOOR LOTE

One of the memories of Ruston which I recall vividly and with fondness is that of the clearing project undertaken in a lot next door when I was in the fifth or sixth grade. In Vedado, the school was seriously handicapped by lack of playgrounds. As I recall it, the building next to the Primary and Intermediate buildings had been torn down but not fully cleared. Permission to use the lot for sports activities had been obtained, but it was up to us to clear out the remaining parts of the building.

This was done by Intermediate students, both boys and girls, during part of our lunch breaks and sports periods over a number of weeks. Remaining pieces of concrete floors were cleared with "mandarias, pico y palas". It was hard work, but to us it was a challenge taken on with great pride. I can remember playing kickball in that lot after the job was completed and the pride that we felt because we had made it happen.

Nora Ostrovsky
Class of 1959

My fondest memory of Ruston is of Dr. Mario Iglesias proclaiming one day to his 6th grade class that since he thought that few of us really knew anything about where we were living, he would donate his time for the next few Saturday mornings to show us around La Habana, the oldest and most historic of American cities.

I don't remember whether we gathered at the old school in Vedado or met at a predetermined point in old Havana, but there were 6 or 8 of us who went. And show us around he did!

We wandered around office buildings ensconced in ancient palaces and "solares" within centuries-old conquistador homes. It was a walking tour to end all walking tours—history on the hoof.

This is a glowing example of teaching at Ruston—unconventional, sometimes seat-of-the-pants, impromptu—but, oh, so effective. And Dr. Iglesias was not even my favorite teacher!

Other instances that come to mind: Gathering water in the pond at the new Ruston for microscopic viewing; Staging plays on the "patios" of both the old and the new schools. So much better than the fancy real theaters my own children had in their American schools.

Some of our best teachers probably would never have qualified for teaching in stateside schools, but, my, were they good! It is a true liking of children and creating enthusiasm for learning in any way possible that makes a really good teacher. And, of course, they were encouraged by a principal who operated in the same free-wheeling way.

Ted Landreth
Class of 1960

Ruston gave me the knowledge and the credentials to get into The Hill School and Harvard, but just as importantly it gave me the confidence to enlist in the Marines, to become a foreign correspondent and bureau manager for UPI at a young age (22), and then a few years later to run the international news operation of CBS News. The most important thing Ruston did for me, though, was to teach me in a way I might never have been taught elsewhere that it was not only possible for me to thrive in a multi-lingual, multi-cultural environment, where everybody's point of view was by definition different from everybody else's—it was the only environment that would make any sense to me throughout my life.

Ruston gave me the best kind of liberal education, in the ancient sense of the word "liberal": it made me try to understand and to love other people for their own sake, and because each one of them was bound to know something that I didn't. Ruston was Cuba for me, and Cuba was Ruston. I was there from 1949 until 1958, through thick and thin, and I remember so much of the experience with such vividness that it is hard to imagine that it all ceased to be 40 years ago. If there is any justice in the world, and any reason, it will rise again soon, with the strongest group of alumni the world has ever known, and I would like to be there with my wife and son and daughter when it does.

Leo (Polo) Núñez
Class of 1961

MY LAST DAY AT RUSTON

During the night of Sunday, April 30, 1961, Castro had launched one of his endless tirades on television. In it, he announced with sound and fury that as of next morning all private schools in Cuba would be nationalized. Upon conclusion of the speech, the television channels concentrated their coverage on the Maine Monument. With much ado, a crane demolished the eagle perching gallantly atop the two columns. It was about midnight; the mob shouted the usual anti yankee slogans.

I had watched all those events with anger and fear. The failure of Bay of Pigs; the death by firing squad of so many Cubans during those April days; the wiping-out of the underground movement in Havana, were ominous indicators of the power in this madman's "revolution". Next morning, Monday May 1, I woke-up early; I had decided to go to Ruston.

Upon arriving, we did not enter the driveway, but parked the car on the street in front of the flag poles. I got out and walked approaching the militia-man sitting, metralleta on his lap, in front of the closed doors. I asked him if I could go in. He answered that this now belonged to the people and that I could if I had any business inside. A little bothered and nervous I replied that I had been a student in the school (the school never reopened after invasion day, April 17) and just wanted to speak to the director; he nodded. I opened the door and headed to the office, but there was nobody there. I walked to the adjacent terrace, looked towards the dining room, and saw some people sitting there.

As I paced along the covered walkway, I saw Dr. Mario Iglesias (Mr. Baker, as of January, had appointed Dr. Iglesias headmaster in his absence), the accountant, and the book-keeper. They must have seen me too because Dr. Iglesias got up and rushed towards me. He was clearly concerned, "What are you doing here?" he asked in an agitated tone of voice. Meekly, (it was never easy for me to address Mario Iglesias in any other manner), I stated that I was there to help them in any way I could and added that perhaps he might want me to take out a document or an important memento of the school . . . He interrupted me, "Polo, how can you be so naive? All the school entrances are secured by milicianos. In fact once in, you cannot go out until the interventor arrives and we find out what is going to happen to us and to the school . . . Follow me to the front door." He walked at a steady pace; I followed.

The miliciano was now inside. Dr. Iglesias tried to persuade him to let me out. He stated that I had been a student there and had nothing to do with the running of the school. The militia-man seemed adamant. Via hand gestures, through the greenish glass, I indicated to the person who had driven me that I could not leave. Dr. Iglesias continued talking to the man; I just stood there very tense. After what seemed to me a very long while (it really was not), the miliciano turned to me in a disgruntled manner, lifted his stretched left arm at about waist level and moved his hand forward at the wrist a few times. I did not need any further coaching. I opened the door without even giving any thanks to Dr. Iglesias; got out in a hurry, crossed the short grassy area and got inside the car. I then looked one last time at the façade. Memories raced through my mind: Christmas pageants with Sibyl Baker, student council meetings, "Taming of the Shrew", Virginia Eagan, Gloria Crespo (in the old Ruston), Alicia González-Recio, Margarita Oteiza, Mr. Baker, Boris Goldenberg, Calvin, Serapio . . . As we speeded away I uttered a very wearisome, "So-long for a while".

I never returned. On June 28, 1961, in a rather big hurry (my father had been held in custody earlier in the month), again I had to say, "So-long for a while", this time to my country. As the plane banked to the north I saw down below and to the left the Morro Castle and the entrance to La Bahía; a sense of complete loss and helplessness grabbed hold of me; it has never quite left me. Today the "while" seems endless, but I am a believer. I doubt that any real student of James D. Baker can be anything else. Thus, I know that in a not too distant future there will be a new and better Cuba and Ruston Academy will again be there to offer top-notch education to its youth.

I often pray that I may be granted the gift of walking those hollowed halls again con mi patria libre, democrática y en paz consigo misma . . . Maybe I'll even be able to meet with Dr. Iglesias (he is now associated with Ohio State University) at Ruston Academy and after so many years finally give him much belated thanks.

Edgardo Marill
Class of 1961

The whole process of building the new school and moving it from Calle G was a dream that many of us lived through. I well remember the old school, with crowded passage ways, crossways with vehicle traffic between buildings, limited or no space for physical education activities. Mr. Baker, as leader, and the Board of Ruston had the dream, and we all worked hard in any way we could to help: selling raffle tickets was a major item for me.

Once we moved, we understood the importance of reaching out for a dream of a better place, having the confidence to execute the dream, and then enjoying some of the results. This whole process had an effect on many of us, I would assert.

Uva de Aragón
Class of 1962

RECORDANDO

Si tuviera que enumerar las cosas que aprendí en el Ruston y que más han influído mi vida, comenzaría por decir que hacer un "outline". Lo que me ha ayudado no es saber que los principales temas se ordenan con números romanos, los incisos con letras mayúsculas, etc., etc. sino esa manía que se me ha quedado de escribir siempre los puntos claves de cualquier tema a desarrollar. Ya sea antes de ir a una reunión, dar una clase, hablar en público, escribir un artículo o un ensayo de mayor alcance, siempre anoto, al menos, cuatro ideas claves.

Se me ocurre que en vez de outline, que en español traducimos como contorno, boceto, o perfil—lo cual nos da la pista que el vocablo debe haber sido robado por las letras de las artes plásticas—deberíamos decir inline, porque lo que hacemos en realidad no es trazar las líneas externas, sino el esqueleto, el eje, el centro de un texto.

El ejercicio, sin embargo, tiene efectos más profundos. Nos obliga—o, al menos, a mí me ha obligado—a concretar, a enseriar el pensamiento. No es un logro pequeño si consideramos que a los poetas se nos tilda de andar siempre por las nubes, y si pensamos en lo pronto que somos los cubanos a improvisar. Fijar de antemano las ideas que deseamos desarrollar nos evita irnos por los cerros de Ubeda. En fin, que con menos palabras, décimos más.

Este hábito de hacer outlines se extiende a todos los aspectos de mi vida. Ya sea para organizar un congreso o salir de compras, hago siempre primero un croquis, una especie de guión. En realidad, se trata de organizar bien el tiempo, o, en palabras sajonas, "time management). Y el tiempo, sin duda alguna, es la materia prima, la substancial esencial con que contamos para desarrollar nuestra vida. No es logro pequeño usarlo bien.

Claro que aprendí muchas más cosas en el Ruston. A la Dra. Oteiza debo que me descubriera a Edgar Allan Poe, cuya teoría sobre el cuento corto aún influye mi narrativa. Esa íntima necesidad de entenderlo todo—desde el Quijote hasta el arte barroco, desde la crisis de Irán hasta la política norteamericana—iluminado por la historia, me viene de las clases de Alicia González-Recio. Al Dr. Rusinyol y a la Dra. Beatriz Varela les estoy en deuda por aumentar la pasión por la lengua que debo haber heredado en el DNA y que ya había alimentado en la escuela primaria de Margot Párraga una maravillosa exilada española llamada Gloria Santullano. La anatomía del cuerpo humano, la lógica inefable de una ecuación de álgebra, la misteriosa armonía de un lienzo o una sinfonía, el nombre de los ríos y valles de Cuba fueron descubriéndoseme bajo la guía amorosa de mis maestros.

Muy a menudo los he evocado. En muchas ocasiones de mi vida, especialmente cuando he publicado algún libro o merecido algún galardón literario, he agradecido, tanto públicamente como en lo más recóndito de mi alma, cuánto les debo. Mucho de lo que hoy soy es reflejo de esa educación cuyas tantas lecciones es imposible recoger en estos breves párrafos.

Pero no aprendí tan solo de mis maestros. También de mis compañeros. Quizás de la que más—y tal vez nunca se lo haya dicho—fue de Nancy Kress. Hasta que llegué al Ruston, para cursar en 1956 el Ingreso al Bachillerato, no había tenido ninguna amiga que no fuera católica. Nancy no sólo me enseñó sobre el judaísmo sino que hizo que mi mundo cultural se ensanchara, y que aprendiera otro principio que ha guiado mi vida: a dialogar y a compenetrarme en el orden afectivo con personas con creencias distintas a las mías. No ha sido lección inútil en un mundo cada vez más pluralista.

Otras formas en que los años de estudios en Ruston Academy marcaron mi vida son más difíciles de precisar. En esas aulas y pasillos supe de manera clara que los sueños pueden tornarse realidad. Desde muy niña quería ser escritora. Fue en The Rustonian que vi por vez primera mi nombre en letras de imprenta al calce de un breve texto que se titulaba, como éste que hoy escribo, "Recordando". Como si de alguna forma presagiara que el presente es ya futuro en el momento vivido, al entrar al primer año de bachillerato sentía nostalgia por el curso anterior. Aún recuerdo vivamente la emoción que sentí al ver mi trabajo publicado. Continué escribiendo casi todos los meses en el periódico del colegio, inclusive en el curso de 1959 a 1960 cuando ya me encontraba exiliada en Washington. En una ocasión obtuve el primer lugar en un concurso de cuentos y me premiaron con una vale que me permitía comer todos los hamburgers que deseara en la cafetería del Biltmore. Preferí renunciar a tal banquete por temor a que me hicieran entregar la tarjeta—que guardé por muchos años y debió haberse perdido en alguna mudada—donde constaba como ganadora del concurso. Fue ese modesto principio de mi carrera periodística y literaria un acicate perenne para no abandonar jamás mi vocación literaria. Y así lo he contado en muchas entrevistas.

Estos recuerdos no incluyen, naturalmente, todo lo que debo al Ruston. Quizás, sin embargo, sean un buen punto de partida para que otros reflecccionen sobre esas lecciones de vida aprendidas en las infancia y la adolescencia, y que moldearon para siempre nuestras vida.

Diego Roqué
Class of 1962

There is no way anybody can pay back an education, much less a Ruston one. In my two and a half years at Ruston, I experienced the whole class being challenged and motivated in a very relaxed yet rigorous manner. All teachers were great and there was a great spirit of "compañerismo" among the students. It was also my first experience in a coed classroom which made it all the more pleasant. When I first went in, coming from Belen Jesuit, I thought that I was going to a school where I would be taught a good command of the English language. Little did I know that Ruston was really a unique universe of life transforming experiences where one could grow and mature to become a solid productive citizen. My words will never be able to do the school justice.

Julio C. Pita
Class of 1963

MY LAST SEMESTER AT RUSTON

It was September 1960. Cuba was in turmoil. Fidel Castro had usurped full power and was rapidly transforming all elements of society toward a socialist-communist system. The Agrarian Reform was in full force and private businesses were being confiscated by the government. Rumors abounded that the government would soon establish an educational system where children over the age of 12 would be sent to government controlled schools away from their homes (Patria Potestad). The anti-Yankee rhetoric was gathering strength. The massive exodus of professionals and business leaders was about to begin.

It was in the midst of this uncertainty that my classmates and I began our third year of Bachillerato at Ruston. From the beginning we all knew it was not going to be a normal year. Some teachers had already left the country but in my class of an original group of 25 approximately 20 attended the first day of classes.

As I approached the high school doors the first sight that greeted me was a small green tractor that Ruston was donating for the Agrarian Reform. (If it is of any consolation, it was almost a toy tractor perhaps slightly larger than those used to mow lawns). Also to our surprise a new course had been instituted. It was a political forum in which issues associated with the socio-political changes in Cuba were to be discussed. This weekly class was run and directed by the students in each class. To this date I do not know whether this was an official directive by the government to attempt to indoctrinate the youth in all schools. If this was the intent it certainly did not work within the classrooms at Ruston. What transpired were open and at times heated discussions on the changes that were occurring in Cuba. We discussed openly the lack of freedoms that were already being instituted. In my class the majority of us were in strong opposition to the government but a few defended the measures being taken. For example, I clearly remember in one session we discussed the lack of freedom of the press. Most of us argued that the government controlled and had taken over most of the newspapers, radio and TV stations. A few argued that one could freely buy American newspapers and magazines at Maximo's. (The totalitarian system had obviously not closed its grip yet). Through it all we expressed our opinions in an orderly fashion and with respect. Our Ruston education had taught us to debate but above all to respect differing opinions.

Our class size rapidly dwindled. Every Monday it became a ritual to see who else had left for it appeared that the exodus occurred unannounced and *usually during the weekends. By mid-November a class field trip to a museum in Old Havana was accomplished in two cars. By the end of the semester in mid December only five of us were left: Sergio Megías who came to Miami in early 1961, Jorge Torrente who stayed only to come with the Mariel boatlift, and Eloisa LeRiverend and Ernesto Velarde who as far as I know are still in Cuba. That last day of classes in December 1960 was extremely sad. The school was nearly deserted, the hallways almost empty. The five of us took a final tour of the school as if to bid goodbye. We walked through the Bachillerato hall, through the Commerce and High School classrooms, the Study Hall, Intermediate School and Elementary School areas. There were no more than fifty students left. We knew that we were saying goodbye to the school and perhaps to each other. What we did not anticipate was for how long. I left Cuba on January 9, 1961 and have never returned.*

Nearly 38 years have passed since that last day of school. At least three of my classmates have unfortunately passed away (Armandito Valdés, José Ramón Villavicencio, and Carlos Alberto Zanetti). I have seen some of my classmates at Ruston or other impromptu class reunions. Some have even risked being my patients and one remains one of my closest friends—Humberto González "el bijirita". Not infrequently, however, my thoughts roam to our two classmates who remained behind. What are they doing? What has happened to them in these 38 years? What do they think? Deep in my heart I feel that no matter what has happened we would be able to sit and discuss our points of view with respect, friendship, and warmth for we share the common bond of adolescence together and a Ruston education.

The class of 1963 never had a chance to graduate at Ruston. I harbor the hope and conviction that we will be able to celebrate our 40th alumni reunion at the beautiful campus of Ruston Academy in a post-Castro Cuba

Sheila Irvine
Class of 1966

    I've been trying to pinpoint what it is about Ruston that made it so remarkable. I think most of all, a particular sensibility, exceptional teachers who were very creative and caring and the notion that Ken Campbell told me Mr. Baker told him, "There is no such thing as a poor student."
    Ruston promoted a balanced approach to life and sound pedagogy. I felt my curiosity carefully nurtured and kindled there, while at the same time we were disciplined quite carefully. I still to this day remember my fear of Mrs. Prieto in grade school and the thought of ending up in her office.
    I do recall asking Mrs. Sibert who was teaching us Fifth Grade English at the time, why I had an S—in conduct. She explained that it was because I was loquacious . . . I love words and had no idea what that might be. When I looked it up though, I felt somewhat humbled, but at the same time intrigued by this serious sounding, elegant word. I still chuckle to think of her sense of humor and intelligence in coming up with such a clever and gentle rebuke. It inspired a sense of fun and a greater curiosity about language.
    I also marveled at the way Dr. Iglesias taught us about communism. Those of us who were up to it and interested were tracked in a class of Science and Math in Spanish. We had to come to school on Saturday's to catch up. During this period, so that too much school did not become drudgery, he arranged for us to go on excursions . . . sometimes we went to exhibitions . . . I remember a very interesting one on Russia in Vedado . . . We also visited our friends country houses in different areas of the province when we had finished with our Saturday classes to help us broaden our boundaries.
    Strangely enough, he also had instituted a system whereby we would be obligated to keep the classroom clean—we were spending a great deal more time there. He made it a cardinal rule not to throw paper on the floor rather than in the trash. The penalty for any paper on the floor was a fine of a nickel. When had collected enough nickels he would buy the whole class cokes. Furthermore, we started to grow tomatoes in the little garden off of our 6th grade class. [To this day, my summer is not complete without growing my own.] But, he did it so that we would get some notion of agrarian reform.
    Another highlight of Ruston was the fact that we had so many interesting activities all day long. It seemed as if we spent a great deal of time playing a variety of games, as well as putting on plays and other events at lunchtime. There was always an area, be it a sport or an event at which we might excel.
    And last, but not least, I have always greatly admired the fact that someone had the wisdom to hire Señora Nina to teach us needlework. She taught us rather

sophisticated stitching on a rather high level in 4th or 5th grade. She also taught us Spanish folklore on her #4 bus route, if one was lucky enough to be going to that neighborhood. From that experience I have honored the notion that we are all teachers and learners.

All in all I have many memories of Ruston, not the least of which are the turtles in the pool of the courtyard of Pre-Primary on Quinta. I am to this day fascinated by them.

I have often wondered if Mr. Ruston went to Harvard and whether or not he qualified the Veritas, to Poetae vere soli sciunt. I think it is the poetry that the experience brought out in each of us that made that school experience so marvelous.

And I find it rather amazing that everyone who went there shares these positive feelings about it.

Hilda Luisa Díaz-Perera
Class of 1967

ON "ALLA EN EL FONDO DEL MAR SALADO"

As with other Hispanic children's songs it is difficult to pinpoint the origins or to date this lovely selection. I heard it sung for the first time in Cuba by a Spanish Civil War refugee whom we called Señora Nina and who worked as the chaperone of our schoolbus.

I remember her tall and big, imposing yet elegant, her gray hair piled high on top of her head in a netted bun, always dressed in black, skirts down to her ankles, wearing wide heeled, laced shoes that held her swollen feet tightly as her body slowly and with difficulty lumbered down the school corridors. Sometimes she would stop to catch her breath, wiping her forehead with a small, white lace handkerchief and asked one of us to please help her carry her things to the teachers' lounge.

She spoke beautiful soft Spanish, full of the Castilian "eses", and wore interesting, aristocratic, silver flat rings, on her long, white, tapered fingers.

Señora Nina owned a treasure trove of children's rhymes and games and could make any bus ride too short. She always carried a square, leather book bag that to us children seemed bottomless, filled with an assortment of handy goodies she magically materialized as needed, from candy to cotton swabs, to colored ponytail barrettes, to a round, tiny tin box of liniment to rub on our scraped knees when we fell and hurt ourselves during her recess watch. When we went to her crying, she would hold us very tenderly and we would disappear into the enormous round haven of her bosom.

Why all this explanation? For a long time, after I heard her sing this song, I actually believed she had lived at the bottom of the sea, and that she had met all these wonderful creatures! When my children were born, I sang this song to them, but sometimes I wondered if I had ever really met Señora Nina, everything related to my childhood seemed to be enveloped in an uncertain mist.

Many years later, in Miami while visiting a friend, I heard her Spanish grandmother sing this beautiful, magic song. But she could not remember where she had learned it or from whom. She did give me an extra verse I had never heard, a verse which probably Señora Nina omitted or had forgotten.

It is thus that a simple song like "Allá en el fondo del mar salado", gets handed down, haphazardly, fortuitously, etched in the memory of sounds and smells and people of the original environment.

Guillermo I. Martínez
Class of 1959
Miami Herald, March 2, 2001

Mr. Baker: "Love Cuba and the United States"
He expected us to become good citizens and to respect the rights of others.

Despite almost 25 years as a teacher first and then as headmaster of the best bi-lingual private school in pre-Castro's Cuba, James D. Baker never spoke Spanish fluently. He didn't have an ear for the language. He had difficulty with those harsh double Rs Cubans like to trill. It was not easy for him to deal with Spanish-language syntax, either.

What Mr. Baker did have was a special skill in creating a learning atmosphere where children from kindergarten through 12th grade never thought of themselves as cubanos or americanos, as Catholics, Protestants or Jews. What he had was a love of children, of their potential. He was an American, proud of his heritage and strong in his beliefs and love of country. He also loved Cuba, with all his heart.

To those of us who studied under him, we were all alike. We were students at Ruston Academy, with a goal of going on to college in the United States or to the university in Cuba. The school's credo was to teach us English and Spanish equally well, with an emphasis on where we wanted to go and what we wanted to do after high school.

The academic curriculum was tough, the standards high. Beyond that, Mr. Baker expected us to become good citizens, to respect the rights of others, to appreciate and understand the beauty of democracy, and to love Cuba and the United States equally. He taught all of us that you didn't have to stop loving one to care for the other.

Two flags were always present at school functions: the Cuban flag, next to the American flag. We sang both anthems. We were taught to respect the history and culture of both countries. There were few medals or prizes for achievements at the school. The only award given was to the graduating senior who best exemplified the spirit of democracy and love for things Cuban and American.

Mr. Baker's love for children and Cuba never wavered. When Castro's revolution smothered the island, Mr. Baker was one of the key players in setting up Operation Pedro Pan, a desperate move by Cuban parents to send their unaccompanied children out of the island. He worked with Monsignor Bryan Walsh in Miami, with U.S. Embassy officials in Cuba and with Cuban parents who could not bear the thought of having their children indoctrinated in Marxist schools.

He did this quietly, without publicity. He was never one to seek the limelight. His goal was someday to return to Cuba and re-open the doors to his beloved

Ruston Academy. He always wanted to continue teaching and to try again to bring Cubans and Americans together under one roof with common goals and aspirations.

So high were the standards at Ruston Academy that many graduates attended Ivy League schools or top technical universities. Many students—driven out of Cuba by communism—became important pillars of this community. Others are scattered throughout the United States, Latin America and Europe. Florida International University President Modesto Maidique is a Ruston Academy alumnus. So are attorney George Harper, investment banker Fred Berens, community activist Bernardo Benes and the Rev. William Skilton, Episcopal bishop of South Carolina.

There are others, many others. We all speak English and Spanish. We never think of each other as Americans or Cubans, only as friends, as classmates who shared a beautiful dream while we were growing up together.

Mr. Baker's name came to mind over lunch with a friend last week. The topic was the strained relations between Cubans and non-Cubans in this community. I wondered what Mr. Baker would have told me if I had asked him how to bridge the gap that separates us. I can still hear the first words of his reply: ``Now, chico . . .''

He would have reminded me that we are all alike despite our different backgrounds; that it is not wrong to love two countries or to speak two or more languages well; that we ought to be civil with each other, respect other ideas and be tolerant; and that we work to break down the barriers that separate us and build the bridges that can make this community stronger.

His advice would have been welcomed, as it is needed.

It won't be forthcoming. Mr. Baker died in Los Angeles over the weekend. He was 94. On March 9, many of his students from around the United States will travel to Daytona Beach to pay him our final respects. Our obligation to his memory is to keep trying to bring us closer together here in exile—or in Cuba, one day.

RUSTON IN PICTURES

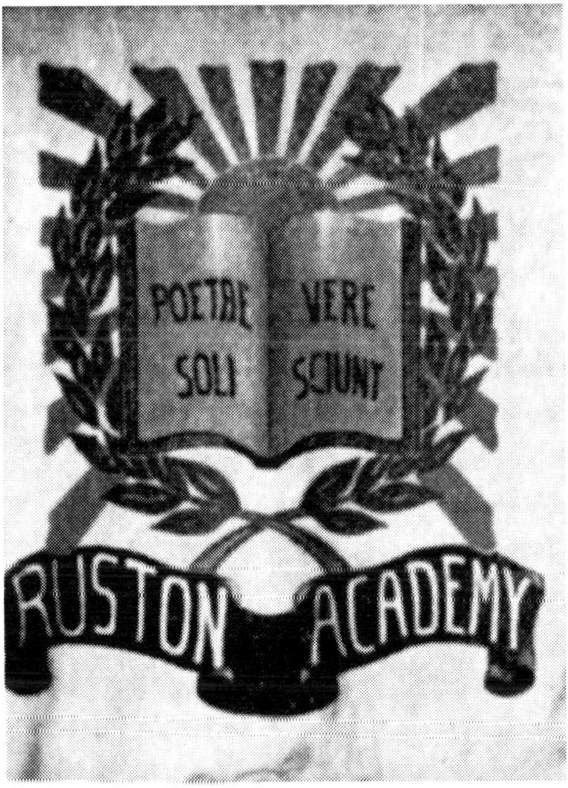
POETAE VERE
SOLI SCIUNT
RUSTON ACADEMY

The Founders

Hiram H. Ruston

Martha Ruston

The Successors

James D. Baker

Sibyl E. Baker

Establishment of the Fundación Ruston-Baker;
Havana, Cuba, 1951

Establishment of the Ruston-Baker
Educational Institution,
Miami, Florida, 1992

128 | James D. Baker

Mr. and Ms. Ruston

Mr. Ruston and Mr. Baker

Mr. Ruston's monthly review of report cards with students

Mr. Ruston and Alumni Association Officers

Ruston | 129

Ms. Ruston

Mr. Ruston at Annual Games
Parque Martí

Sketch of Mr. Ruston by
Emilio Lorenzo

Ms. Ruston's birthday celebration

130 | James D. Baker

First home of Ruston Academy in Marianao, 1920

Aerial views of the area around the second home of
Ruston Academy in Vedado, 1921-1955

Building located at corner of G y Quinta in Vedado, 1921-1955

Primary and Intermediate Buildings located across the street from Main Building

Science Building located half a block north of the Main Building

Bachillerato Building located one block west of the Main Building

Ruston views

Ruston | 133

The porch of the Main Building—study hall, classroom, dining room, and general meeting place

The patios

Ruston | 135

Patio activities

First day of school

Ruston | 137

Primary school, 1941

Kindergarten and Pre-Primary, 1951

Primary and Intermediate activities

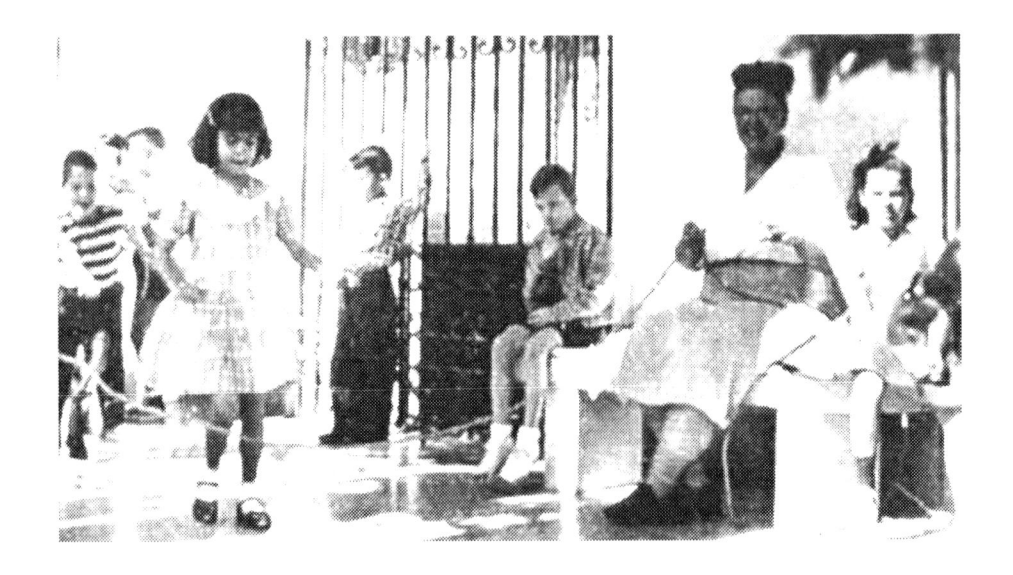

Ruston | 139

Smallpox vaccinations

Orange Crush field trip

Periódico El Mundo field trip

Art

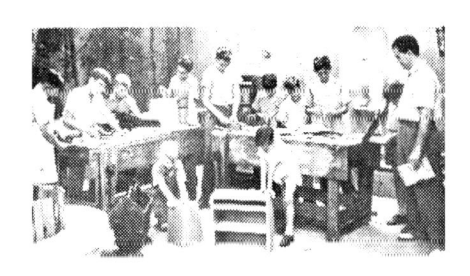

Carpentry

Leatherwork

Sewing

140 | James D. Baker

Ceremony honoring memory of José Martí

Ruston | 141

Life in the Upper School

142 | James D. Baker

Recreo en el Malecón

Waves at the Malecón

Results

Recess activities

Ruston dances

Ruston | 145

146 | James D. Baker

Lunch time at Ruston

Teachers at work

148 | James D. Baker

School excursions

Ruston movie night stage show

James D. Baker

Upper School sports

Ruston | 151

152 | James D. Baker

Theater in the patio

Ruston | 153

Julius Caesar

Much Ado About Nothing

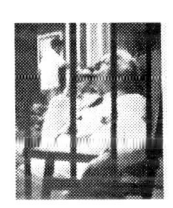

Sketch by Frances Sutton

El Niño Inválido by Ruston teacher
Antonio Vázquez Gallo

Vive Como Quieras

Ruston | 155

Choirs at work

Girls' Choir

Boys' Choir

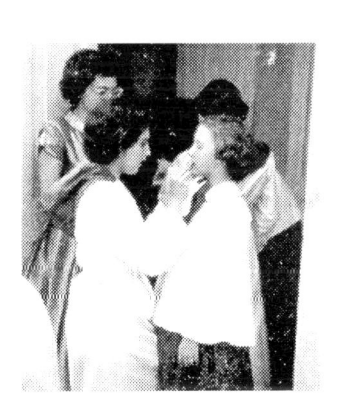

Junior Choir

Senior Choir

James D. Baker

Graduation at the Community House

THE RUSTONIAN

THE RUSTONIAN is published monthly in Ruston Academy.

PRICE 10c

VOL. 10   HAVANA, CUBA - MAY 30, 1951   No. 9

IT PAYS TO DREAM

Before 1920 a very wise man had a great dream, a dream of creating a school that would employ new methods of guiding the development of each student toward a fuller realization of the potentialities of his mind, character, personality, and service as a citizen. He devoted twenty-six years of his life to making his dream come true. Because some of us who had the rare privilege of working with him caught this vision, we too dedicated ourselves to working for his ideal. Our school today is a tribute to the greatness of Mr. Ruston, and a convincing proof that dreams can become realities.

A few days ago, another dream came true.

When I returned to Havana in 1944, it seemed to me that an important protection was needed to make permanent Mr. Ruston's achievement. The ideals of this school and the things we work for are too big and too vital to depend upon one individual owner. Mr. Ruston's dream belongs to the future, and the organization which carries it out should be permanent. For seven years I have looked forward to the day when the school could be changed to a non-profit foundation.

On April twenty-seventh, Mrs. Baker and I had the deep satisfaction of giving our ownership of the school to the Board of Directors.

Ruston is now established to carry on the tradition of some of the great private schools and universities of the United States by devoting all its energies to building an ever-improving school. Whatever gifts she may receive, whatever profits she may make, will go not to an individual owner, but to making it possible to render fuller service to her students, to Cuba, and to your world of tomorrow.

Before school is closed in June, we hope to be able to complete the purchase of land for our new building. Then we shall be one step nearer to the realization of that dream so important to all of us—the completion of a plant with modern facilities, ample playgrounds and sport fields—that physical monument which we shall build to Mr. Ruston's memory.

It pays to dream dreams if we are willing to plan carefully, work hard, and have enough faith in our vision not to become discouraged by delays. What Mr. Ruston did, what we are doing today, you too can do. Your world and the progress of the future will depend very much upon the kind of dreams to which you dedicate your lives.

                                    J. D. Baker.

James D. Baker

New Ruston Academy in Alturas del Country Club, 1955-1961

Ruston | 159

New Ruston under construction

James D. Baker

THE OLD   AND   THE NEW

THE COLUMNS

About three years ago a change of name was suggested for the yearbook. Few people understood and fewer remembered what **The Columns** stood for. But the change was never made; there was something meaningful about **The Columns**, something few ever thought about, yet something everyone had experienced.

The Columns came from the Old School. There, among the tall ceilings and thick walls, stood the solid pillars. They were impervious to change; they were symbols of a faith which never has been nor ever shall be forgotten. They stood as supports for roofs over tiled porches, and they stood also for the belief in youth educated in the principles of freedom and liberty for all. Somehow, in their mighty construction, they expressed a hope for the future — a hope for a world of peace where practicality and idealism might work together for the betterment of mankind.

In the new school the inspiring columns were missing. They had been replaced with slender supports of functional architecture. At the time, no one realized that the new structure carried a meaning of its own. Here was a symbol of true accomplishment. Here, through the work of many men and women, strong in their desire for a new building, was the realization of the faith inherent in the Old School columns. The new home, like the old one, embodies the Ruston ideal.

And thus the faith persists as it always shall. Young men and women study and graduate; they go out into a world they are prepared to meet. They carry with them the faith which can never be surpressed. The columns live on forever.

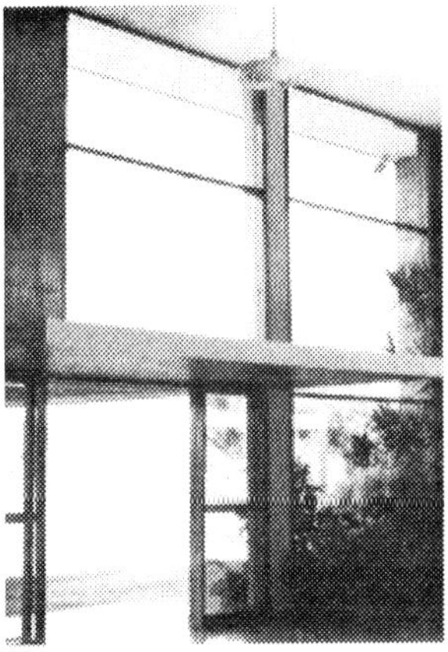

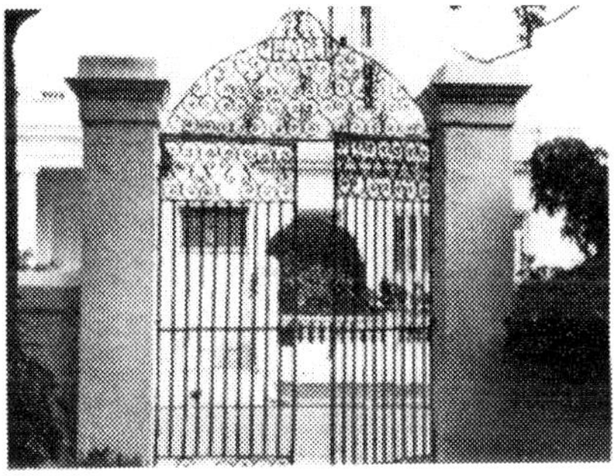

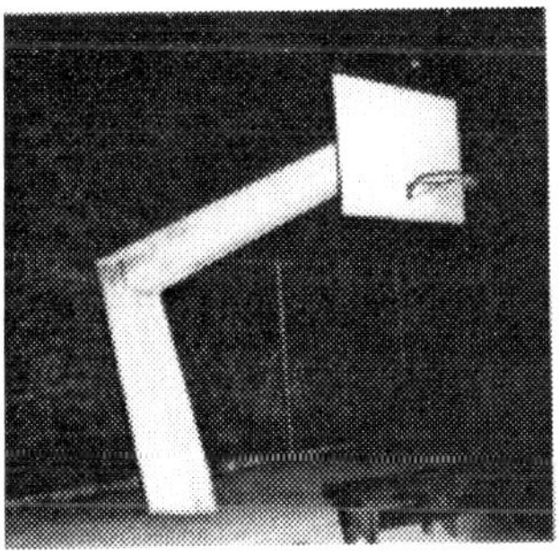

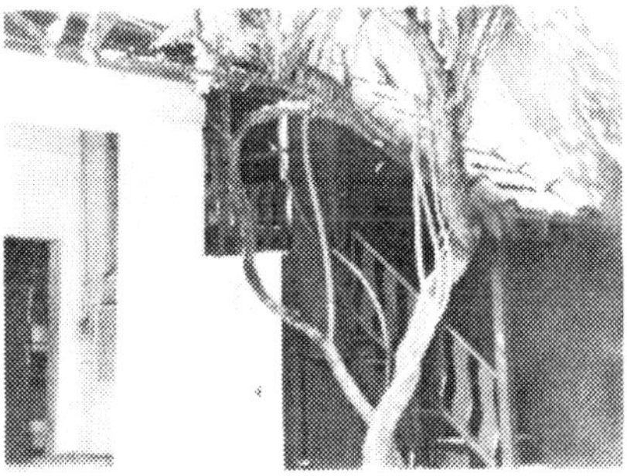

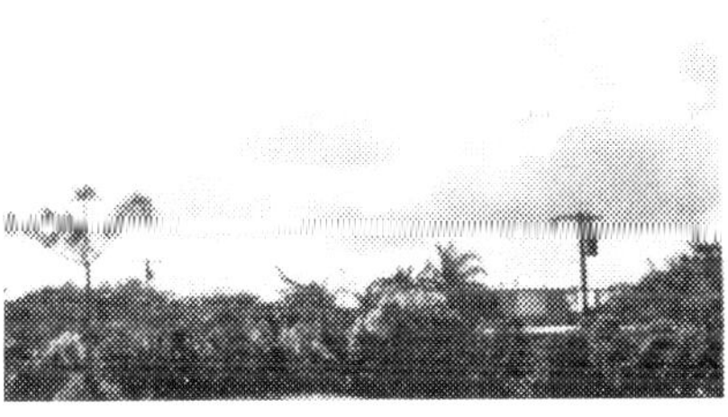

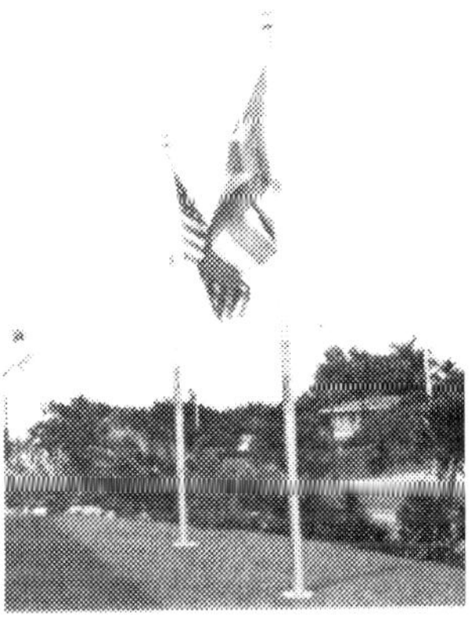

Hiram H. Ruston Memorial Fountain

Ruston | 163

Dawn comes to the new Ruston Academy

Getting ready to open

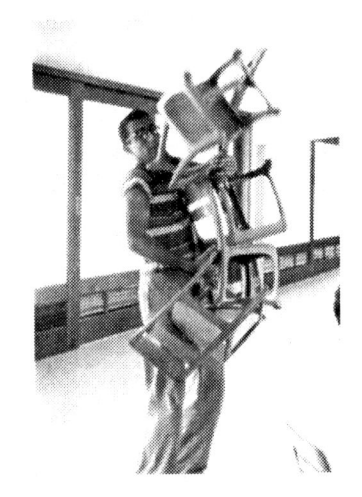

Ruston | 165

Familiar scenes

James D. Baker

Ruston | 167

168 | James D. Baker

Ruston | 169

170 | James D. Baker

Ruston | 171

First day of school

Primary and Intermediate at work, rest and play

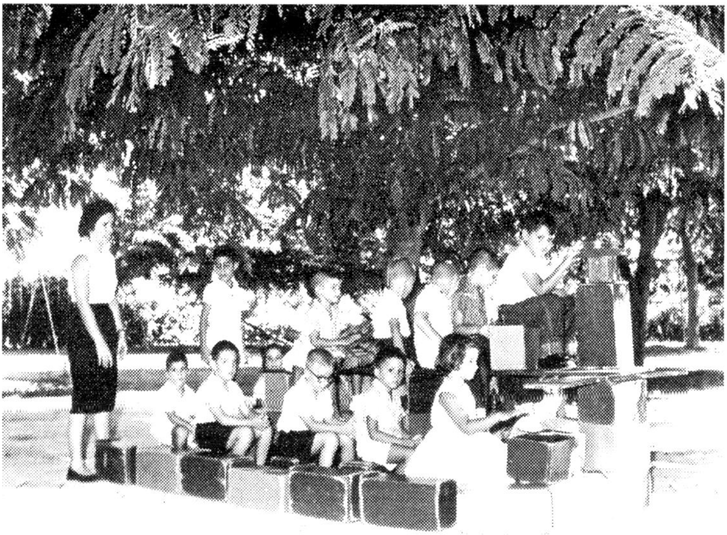

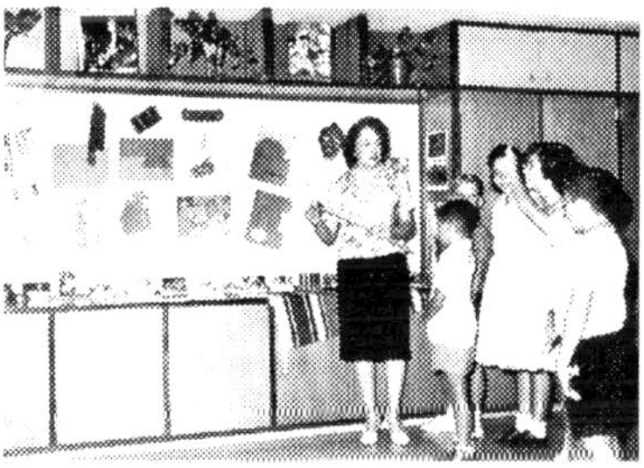

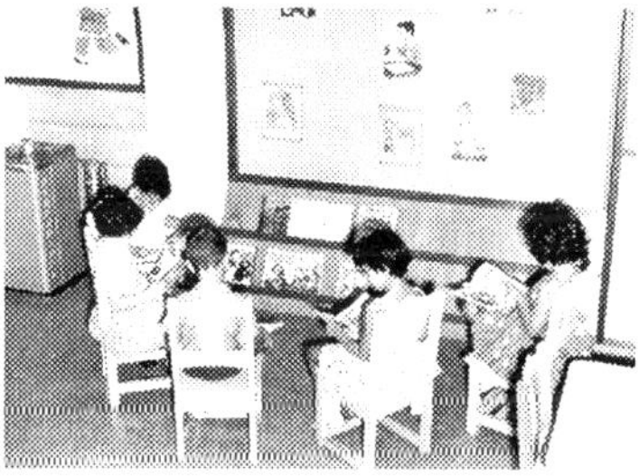

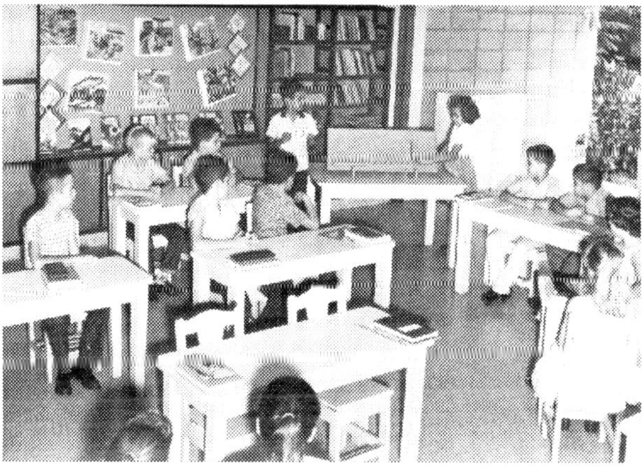

174 | James D. Baker

Steel band comes to Ruston

Pachanga time at Ruston

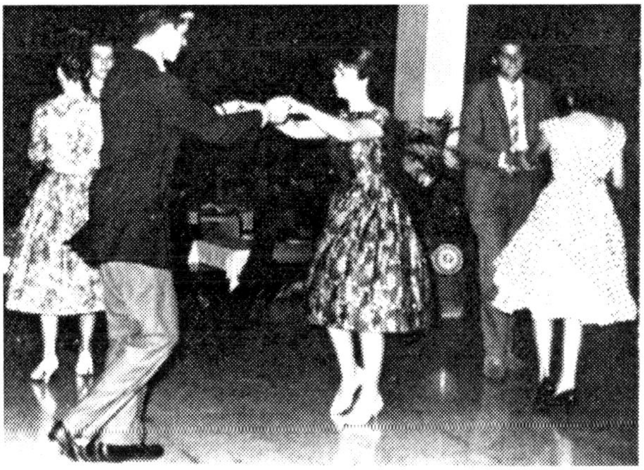

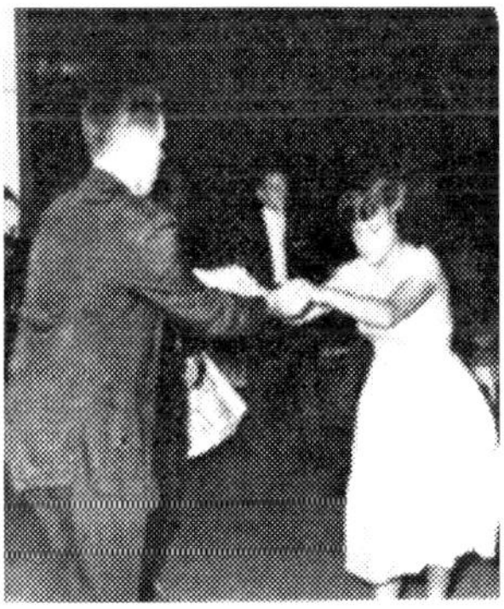

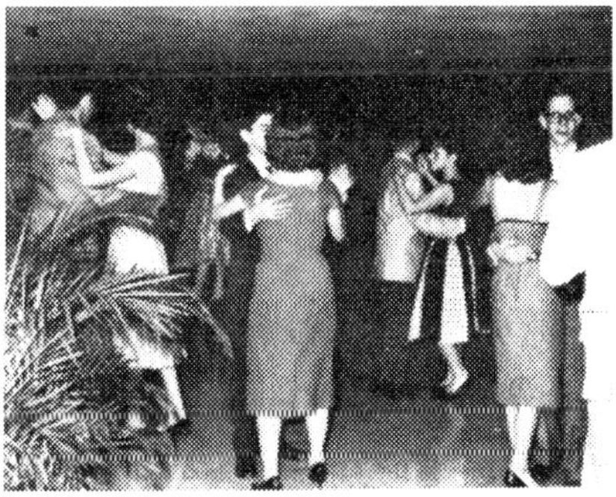

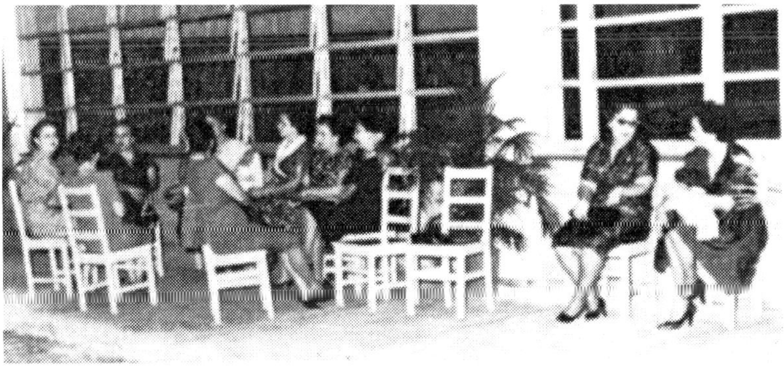

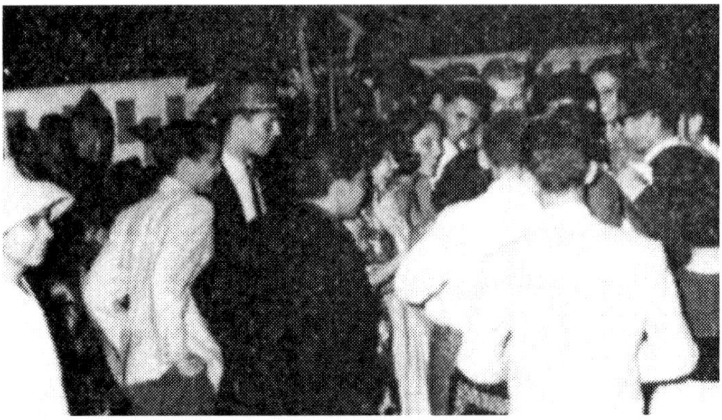

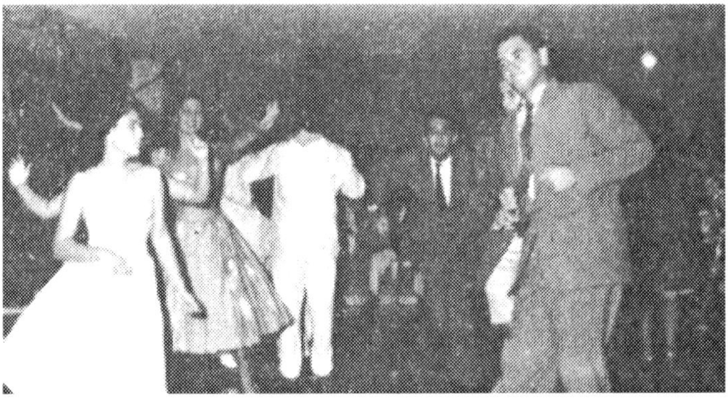

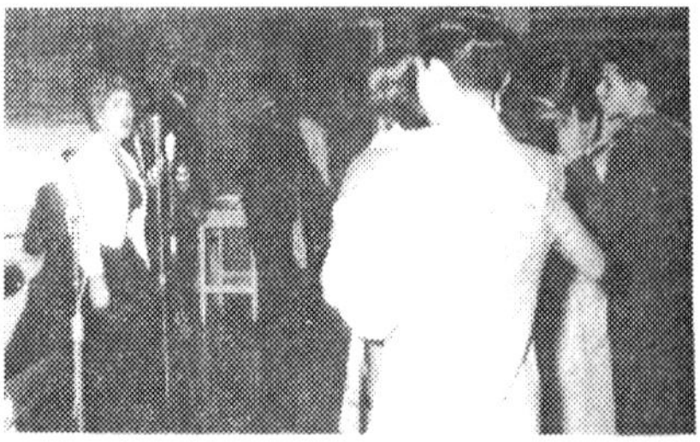

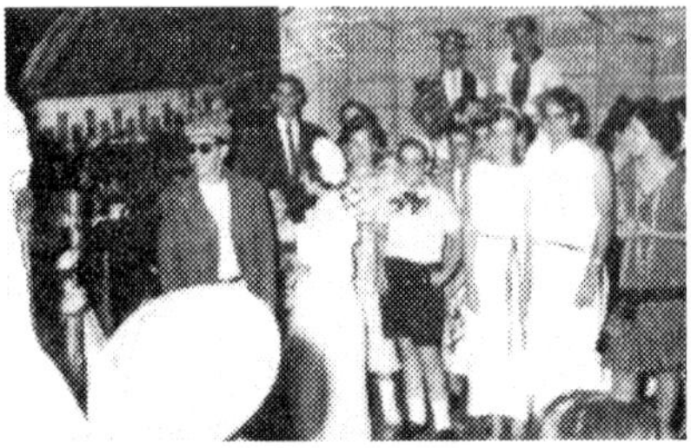

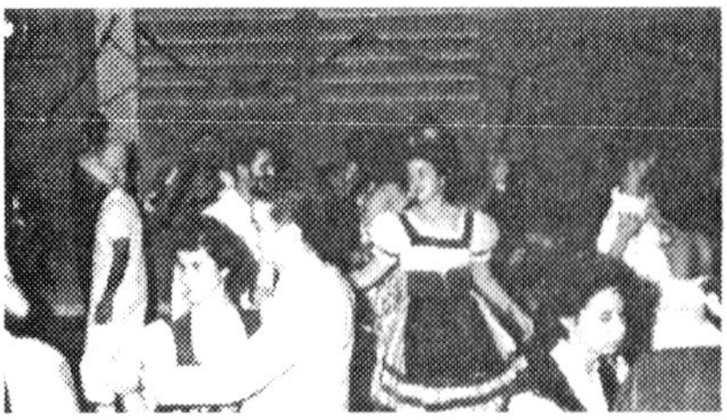

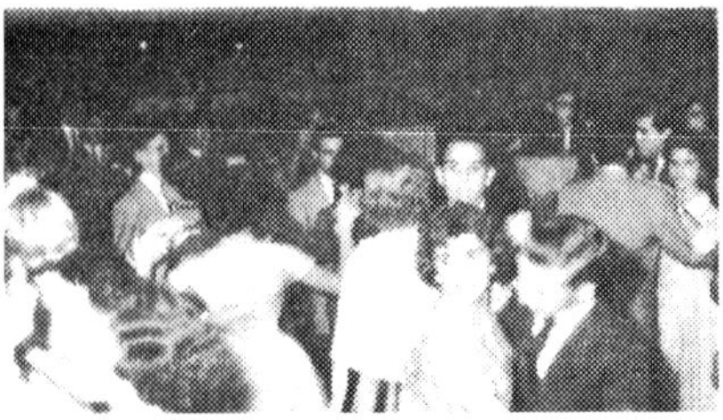

Ruston | 179

Break times at Ruston

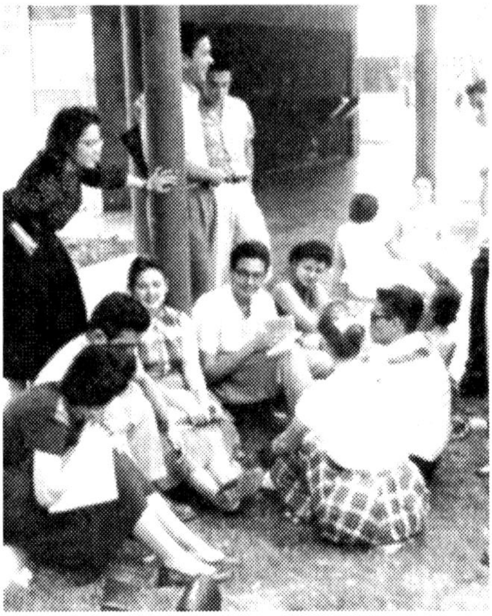

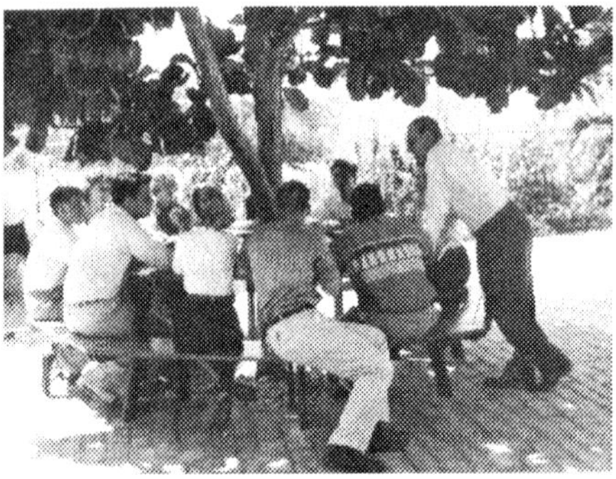

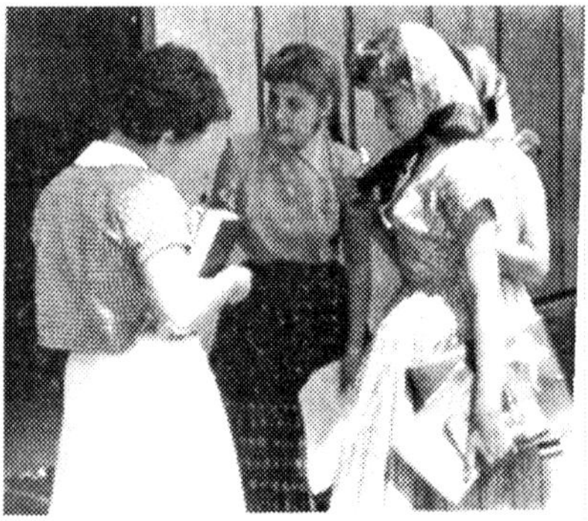

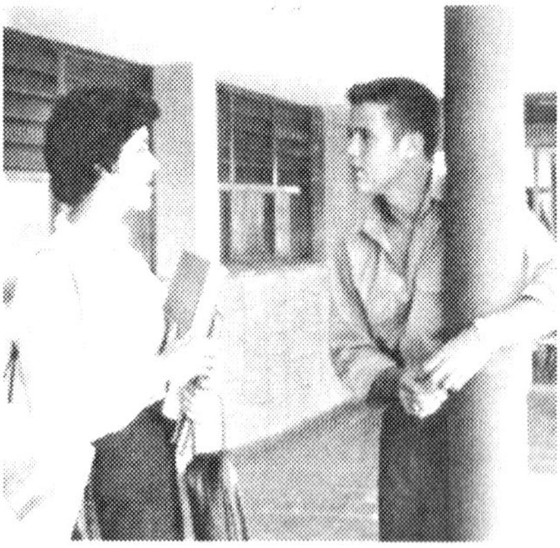

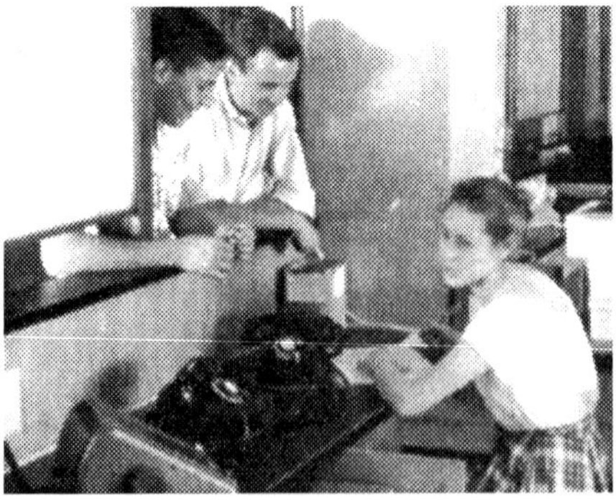

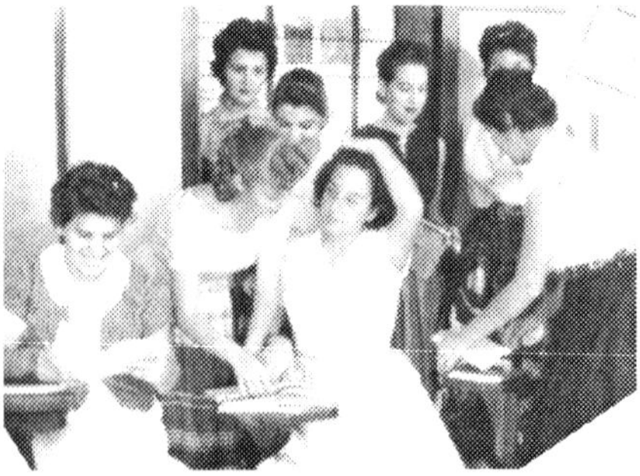

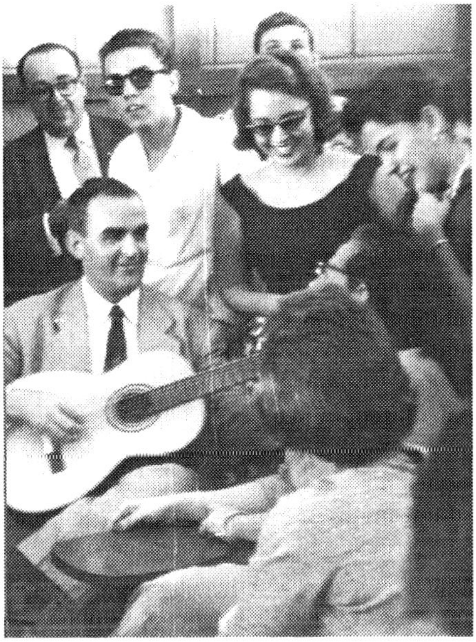

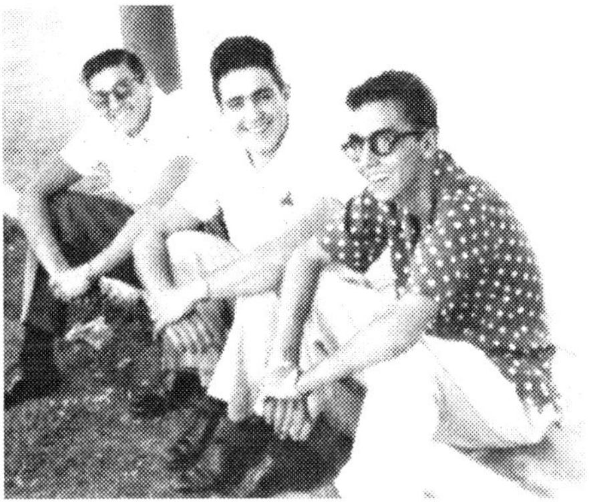

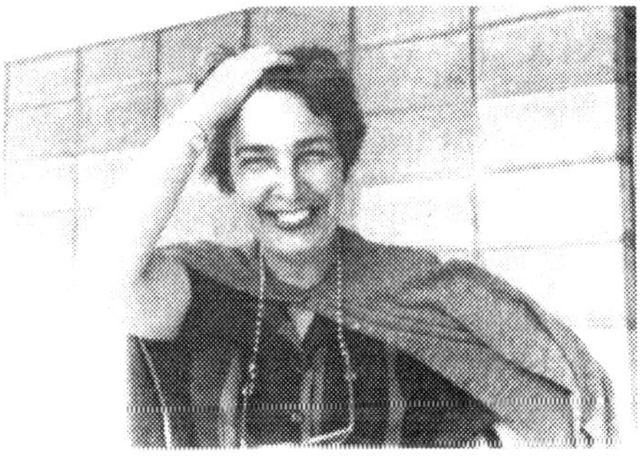

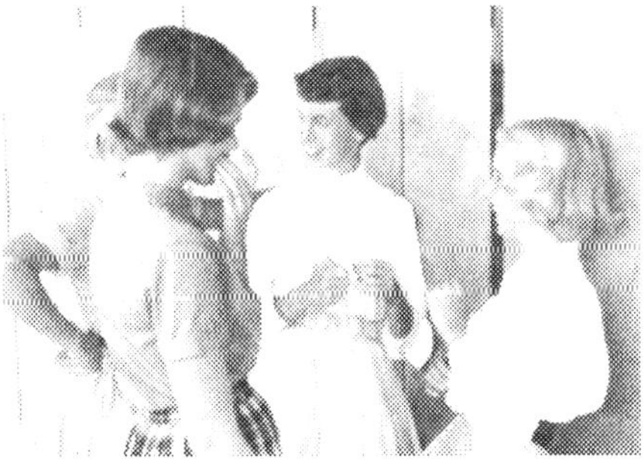

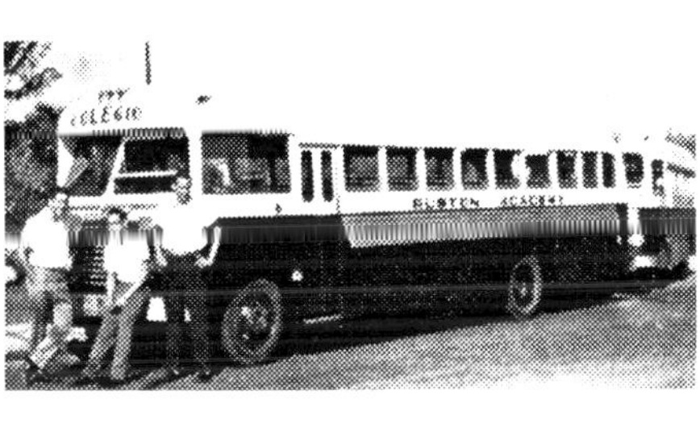

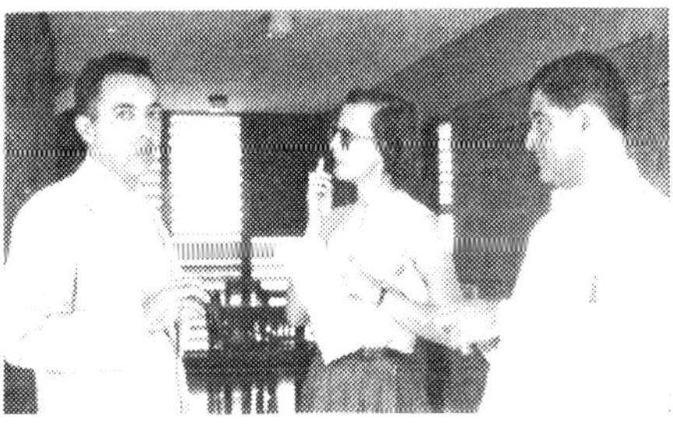

Movie night stage show

Ruston | 183

Boys' baseball team

Boys' basketball team

Girls' volleyball team

Girls' kickball team

Girls' basketball team

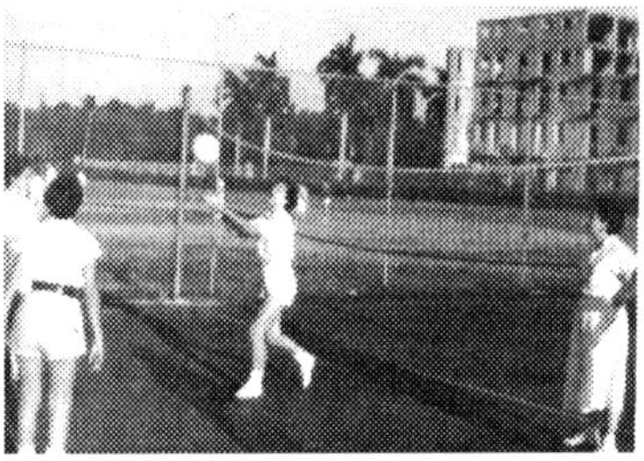
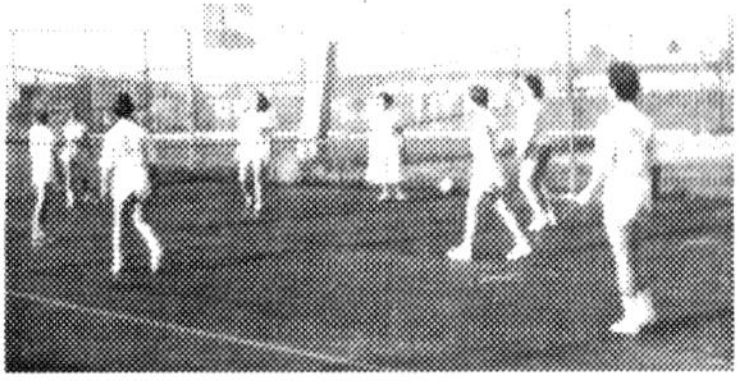
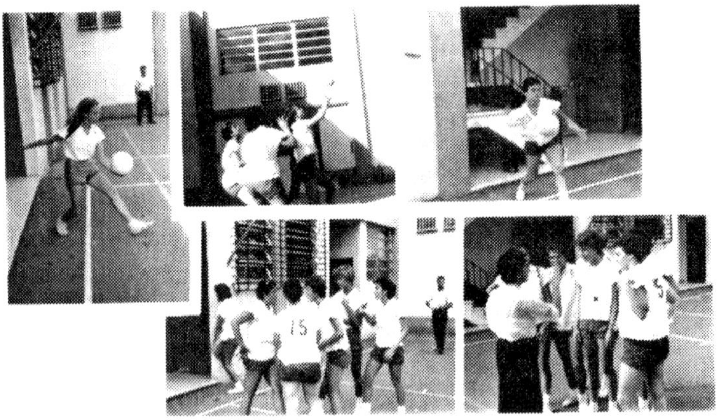
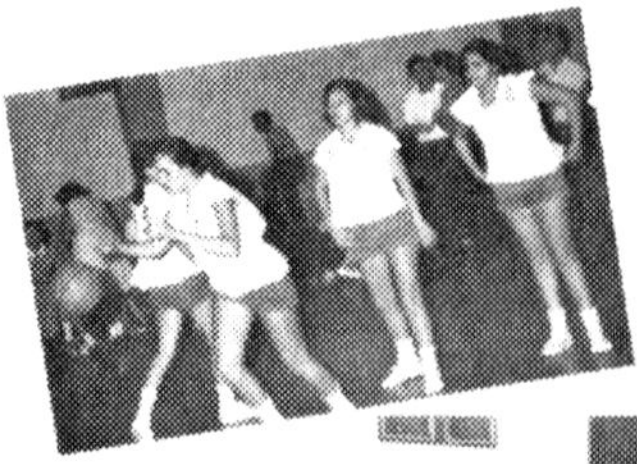
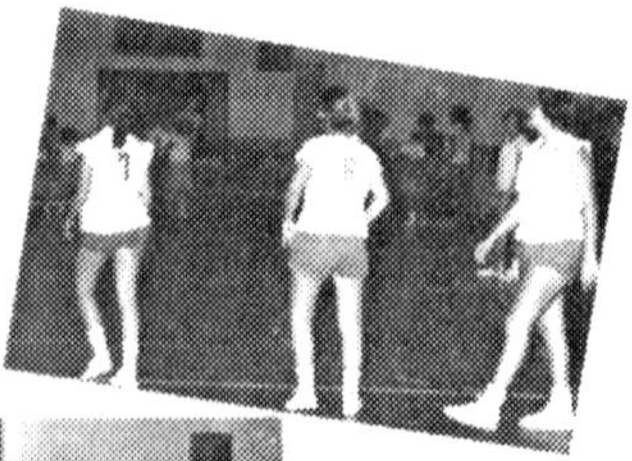
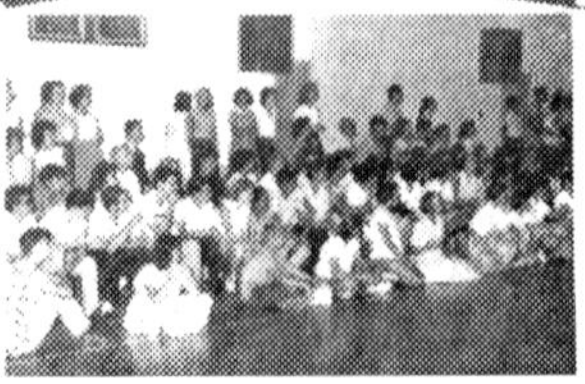

Ruston | 187

Student-faculty games

Helping hands

Much Ado About Nothing

Prohibido Suicidarse en Primavera

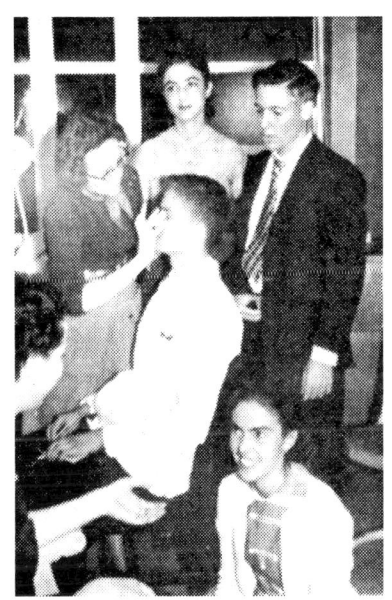

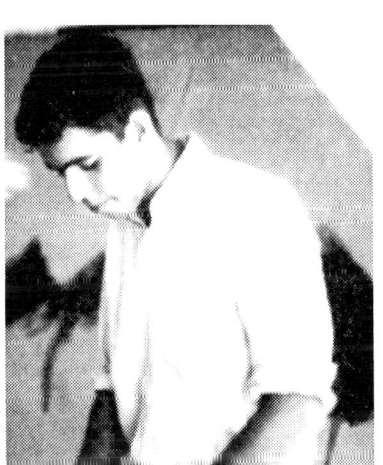

Junior Choir

Ruston | 193

Madrigal Choir

Senior Choir

James D. Baker

Graduation

Ruston Reunions

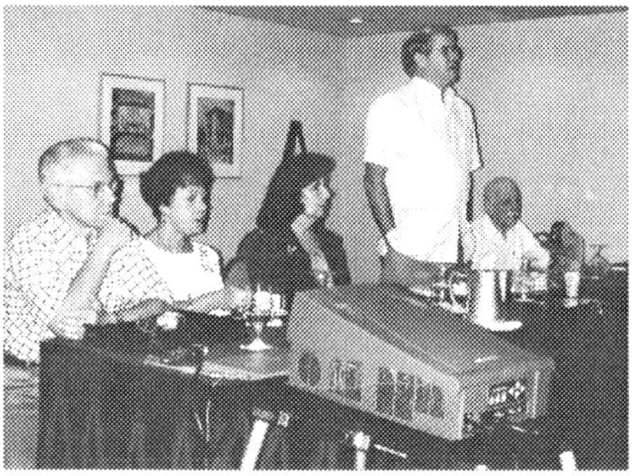

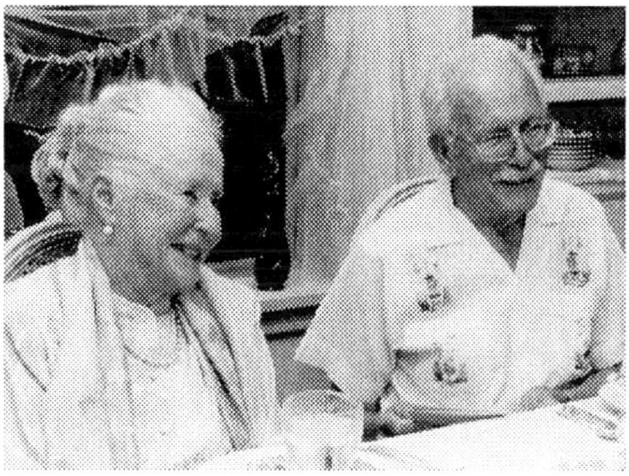

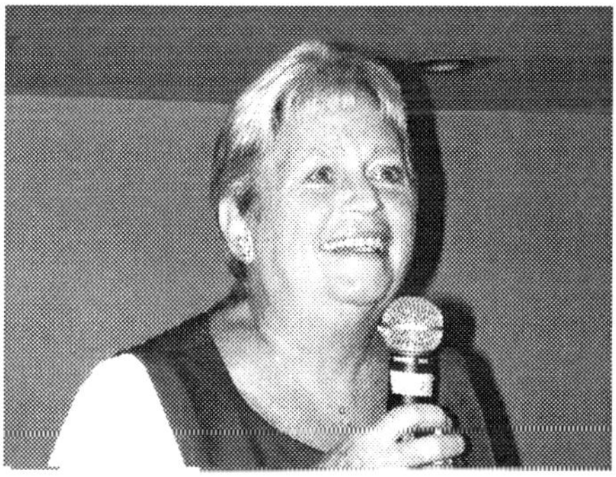

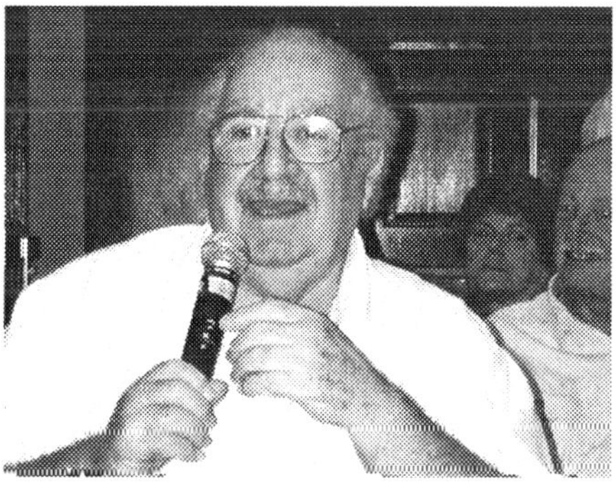

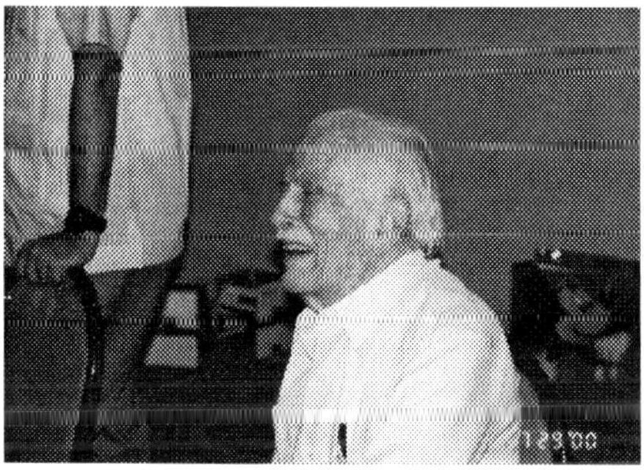

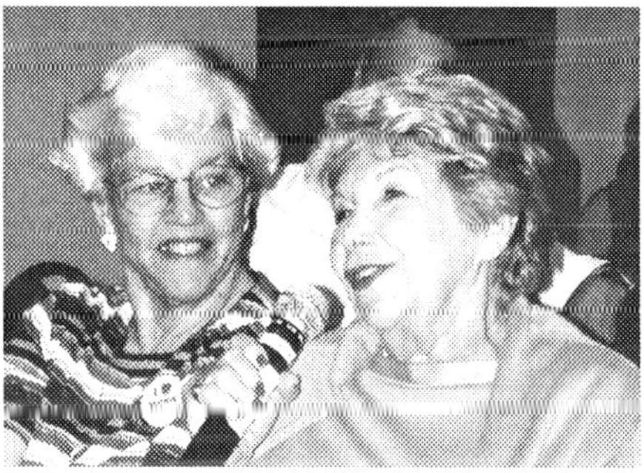